MY BROTHER'S KEEPER

by

Arthur Guy

Acknowledgements

First and foremost, I dedicate this book to the only person I love more than me: Martha Jones.

Secondly, I acknowledge Thomas Moyler aka Gutta for letting me in his lane on this book/publishing shit. I preciate it FAM RS!

Family First:

* To my pops Arthur Sr. Love and my siblings Shakita, Kim, Tierra, T, Mike, and Michiko: Stay safe and I love y'all

* To my nieces and nephews Essence, Zay, Kahri, Serenity, Trinity, Jo-Jo, Noah, Amazin, Ladybug, Siah, Tooley, Majesty, Jatavia, Kentario, Miranda, Lil T, Shareef, and Madison: continue to be happy

* Grandma Dollbae and Grandma Pretty Mae: thanks for passing down y'all strength

* To my aunts and uncles, I send my love, especially to Aunt Monzola, Uncle George, and Uncle Earl: continue to rest in peace and watch over the fam

* To my cuzzos and everybody else whose blood runs thru my veins: I would get a headache trynna name everybody but I love y'all all the same

* To my cousin George Jr.: Rest in peace

My Dawgs

* Rah Black, Ant Caesar, and Ray: Stay up

* Lil man, Tye, Marcus, Boogie, and Chase-o: Stay tough and I love y'all niggas

* Row, Bud, Mal, 40, J-Real, Marcel, Red Bricks, Skrilla, Smoke, Steve, Jazz-o, T-rose, Fattz, Dre narwood, Tone frm hpt, Hotboy, Sha Blaq, Mink coat, Tito, Fly, Foe, Spinoza, Woodah, Ced, Tito and everybody else I rock wit: y'all already know

* To Lump and C-Thugga: stay focused out there and I love y'all niggas, word

To end this jaint I say to my dawgs in the trenches: Everything happens for a reason and nothing lasts forever, so stay thuggin and bossed up and we gone be aiight... RIP Brandon Peterson and Rodney Swain

Ajizzle

Chapter 1

"Damn, dawg, do you gotta be so fucking loud?"

"Man, just find the button for the trunk." Gotti hit the switch releasing the trunk of the Mercedes LS430. He dreamed many times of driving the foreign car to a club escorted by an exotic female and a pocket full of money. Unfortunately the reality was at sixteen, broke, with no food and a mom who could care less whether they had any coming, he and his younger brother Gutta had to do what they could to survive. Currently grand larceny was the motive. They had been breaking and entering cars all night in the Hampton suburb. Their ambition was to stumble upon enough change to guarantee they wouldn't go to sleep hungry for the second night in a row. Recently that had become the norm for the brothers since their mother, Tina, was fired from her job as dispatch for the Porters Cab Company. Unemployment pushed her over the line from smoker to full-fledged crack addict. Food was scarce, money short, and love was nowhere to be found.

Gotti felt his mind begin to slip. Snapping from his state of depression, he revisited his current task. Right now he was elbow-deep under the 430's passenger seat, searching for whatever currency was available. A light chuckle escaped his lips. He heard his little brother, head-first in the Benz trunk, cursing like he was on leave from the U.S. Navy. "Fuck this dumb ass shit" and "I'm tired of this bullshit" was all he could manage. "Ayo, bruh, you find something?" Gotti burst into laughter, already knowing the answer.

"Nigga, do it look like I found something? You always joking and shit." He was clearly frustrated.

"Stop bitching."

"Man, whatever, I'm done. How bout that?" Gutta was beginning to give up hope that he might actually eat tonight when, out of nowhere, he noticed a shiny object under the car's spare tire. All 32 pearly whites displayed as Gutta realized what he uncovered. "Ay brah!" he yelled.

"What!" Gotti jumped up as if the police were coming.

"Look." Gutta pointed the gun at Gotti like he was a member of SWAT.

"What the fuck you doing, fam? Don't point that shit at me." Gotti snatched the gun from his lil brother. Oozing with excitement, he admired the all-chrome P90 Ruger. He always viewed the gangsters from his hood with guns tucked in their waistband, but never had the privilege of holding one of his own. He couldn't deny the power and feel of invincibility. It was enticing for him to keep the gun, but hunger spoke to him in ways he was all too familiar with.

"My nigga, we can get at least two hundred for that," Gutta said.

"Who we gone sell it to, though?"

"It don't even matter. I'm trynna hit Golden Corral off this shit." Gutta was fed up with the mediocre food at McDonald's. The promise of an all-you-can-eat Golden Corral buffet was a welcomed proposition. "Let's go out the hood and sell it."

The brothers walked down the street towards the bus heading to Newport News. They couldn't help but admire and be amazed at the colossal-sized houses out Farmington. Farmington Estates was a housing neighborhood in Hampton, Va, where all the mini mansions were located. The neighborhood was filled with the extravagant homes of doctors, lawyers, and judges. Living in a place such as this wasn't even in the realm of possibility for the brothers. It seemed like a lifetime away from the Marshall Courts projects they called home for as long as they could remember.

The entire bus ride the pair rode in silence, lost in their daydreams. After arriving at the projects, the brothers decided to stop by their house to contemplate who they could sell the gun to. They would have to be careful not to choose someone who would try to take it without paying them. Neither brother was timid or scared of any of the hoodlums who hung out in the projects. The only problem was to the seasoned gangsters who posted on the block smoking weed and selling crack, they were considered children. Gotti, being the oldest, only stood about five feet eight inches tall and weighed about 150 pounds soaking wet with Timberland boots on. His dark-chocolate skin complexion and thick waves were the only things he had going for himself. Unfortunately none of those attributes would do any justice if a full-sized adult wanted to strong-arm him. His brother, being about two inches shorter and ten pounds lighter, wouldn't be of much assistance either. Fully aware of their shortcomings, the brothers knew they had to be smart while making their decision on who to solicit the Ruger to.

"Man, I'm hungry as shit." Gutta entered the apartment, beelining straight to the kitchen. Hopeful, he opened the refrigerator door, only to find a life full of disappointment. The desolate icebox housed a jar of mustard, a jug of Kool-Aid, and a box of baking soda. He slammed the door shut. Turning towards the pantry, he grabbed the last few slices of bread. Anything would have to suffice in quieting the rumbling of his stomach. Entering the living room, he plopped down on the sofa and spectated as his brother analyzed the P90. The sheer weight of the object mesmerized Gotti. Out of the blue he popped up, running upstairs. "That nigga bugging." Gutta shook his head and grabbed the TV remote.

After ten minutes of the local news, Gotti came downstairs with the same speed and urgency as he went up. "Bruh, I got three dollars. What's up?" Gotti held the three one-dollar bills out for his little brother to see.

"Where you get that?" Gutta asked.

"I forgot I got it from dude mom had over here last night."

"That's aiiight. Let's go to Leon's and get some chips and shit."

"Bet then we can holla at Marco and see if he trynna cop this gun."

The duo diddy-bopped up the 36th Street sidewalk. Their destination was the local corner store. Growing up in the streets provided the brothers with a certain bodacious swagger. Today that swagger was on full display. As they approached Leon's they noticed Marco posted by the entrance with a gang of nickel-and-dime hustlers. Marco was a 30-year-old petty drug dealer who made his fortune doing hand-to-hand deals on the street. He was successful as a hustler but far less successful when it came to saving his money. Almost fifteen years in the narcotic business and he barely had enough cash saved to pay for a lawyer. "What's up, Marco," Gotti greeted the part-time hustler with a dap. Gutta stood close by with the look of a cold killer on his face.

"Sup, lil nigga."

"Yo, I came upon something you might want to look at."

"Fuck you talking bout, fam?"

Gotti leaned in so only Marco could hear. "I got a burner for sale."

"No bullshit? Let me see it."

Gotti hesitated. "I need two hundred for it, though."

"Aight, I said let me see it. You know I'm up out here. Stop playin." Marco flaunted his egotistical attitude.

After a little more hesitation, Gotti surveyed the area to assure the cops weren't about to ride past. Seeing that the coast was clear, he reached under his shirt, pulling the Ruger out like it was a Japanese sword. "Damn, that shit tough. Give it here," Marco said, reaching for the gun.

Mindful of how cruddy the dudes on the block could get, Gotti snatched the gun away and took a step back. "Where the two hundred at?"

"Lil nigga, I got that bag out here. You talking bout a punk-ass two hundred dollars. Let me see that shit before I buy it," Marco barked. He was obviously vexed at the lack of respect he felt he was getting from Gotti.

Gutta, noticing how heated the situation was, stepped up in an attempt to calm both parties. "Look, Marco. We don't want no smoke. We just trynna get something to eat. Just give him the bread first."

"Fuck y'all niggas. I'd rather give my two hundred to yo crackhead ass momma for some of that bomb ass head." Marco had venom in his tone when he spoke.

Gotti couldn't believe what he was hearing. The blatant disrespect infuriated him. His vision started to fade in and out. All he could focus on was the group of hustlers laughing like Kevin Hart was performing. Marco's words stung his ears over and over. The dripping of his younger brother's tears reverberated in his soul. Suddenly the world went black and he snapped. The power engulfed his senses as he aimed the barrel of the P90.

The block went silent. Marco's audience began backpedaling to the street, making room for him, Gotti, and the monstrous pistol. His eyes carried the look of death. "Put that shit away before you make a mistake, lil nigga." Marco matched his gaze.

Gotti felt like a caged animal yearning for freedom. The entire hood scrutinized the scene, waiting for him to either react or back down. "Fuck it." He squeezed the trigger three times, sending two bullets to Marco's chest and one to his head. Death greeted Marco instantly. His body collapsed like the Twin Towers, sending the projects into a frenzy. The screams could be heard for blocks. "Come on, let's go." Gutta pulled Gotti's arm, snatching him from his daze.

The brothers ran full speed to their apartment. Once inside, they locked the doors and closed the blinds on the windows. "What the fuck, brah?" Gutta's arms were raised in the air.

"Fuck that nigga." Gotti nervously paced the floor. Even though Marco was surely burning in hell by now, the situation had him vexed to the point it was hard to sit still. He couldn't fathom why Marco put his back against the wall like that. It was like he was begging for death. Either way, he had to teach him a lesson. By the way it sounded when the bullets shredded his torso, he could tell it was a lesson learned.

"Sit down, Gotti, damn!" Gutta was also nervous, but the sight of his brother walking back and forth was doing little to de-escalate the built-up tension.

Gotti took a deep breath and exhaled as he flopped down on the couch. The brothers sat in silence. They could hear what seemed like hundreds of sirens from multiple police cars speeding to the scene of the crime. Neither one could wrap his mind fully around what had just transpired at the store.

Gutta, not wanting to break the silence but knowing he needed to get out of the house, looked over at his brother. "You still hungry? Give me the money so I can go get some chips from the other store."

"Aight." Gotti handed his brother the three singles from his pocket. "Be safe out there." Gotti put emphasis on his words so his brother knew the importance of his request.

Gutta threw on his black Champion hoodie, zipped it up, and proceeded towards the door. He took a deep breath, preparing himself for what might await him on the other side. He began departing when Gotti called his name, stopping him in mid-stride. "Gutta."

"Wassup, brah?" Gutta replied, turning to face his brother.

"Love you, my nigga."

Gutta embraced his brother's sentiments. Not wanting to get emotional, Gutta replied simply, "Already." He then threw the hood of his hoodie over his head, pulled the strings, and left.

As soon as he stepped outside, he noticed the projects was still buzzing with activity. It was a windy summer day, so of course everybody in the neighborhood was out and about. Not to mention a crime scene always seemed to attract the attention of the nosy residents. Gutta stepped to the curb, glancing towards Leon's. He noticed Marco's corpse had already been picked up and the crowd was starting to disperse. All besides the stragglers who were left behind to pick up whatever information so they could spread the gossip later. Gutta shook his head before starting on his journey to 35th Street and Madison Avenue, where the next closest corner store was located.

Along the way he decided to stop by Ebony's apartment to detect whether she was aware of the events of earlier. He and Ebony had been friends for as long as he could remember. She, being ten years his senior with three kids, knew a relationship between them wouldn't work. Since she was the one to take his virginity, she would always be a willing participant whenever he wanted to practice, as she called their lovemaking sessions.

Gutta approached her stoop, observing the curious stares of the little kids across the walkway from Ebony's apartment. He chuckled, knowing the boys meant him no harm. They probably just had a ton of questions and either knew it wasn't the right time to ask or were just too scared.

He knocked on the door three times before she answered. At five feet six inches, with mocha-colored skin and 34-25-42 measurements, she could easily pass for a *Smooth* magazine cover shoot model. Immediately he noticed she had an attitude. "Damn, wassup, shorty?"

She marched away from the door. Gutta admired her plump derriere that hung out the bottom of her t-shirt. "Wassup hell! Why y'all do that to Marco?"

Gutta laughed. It was amazing how fast word spread in the hood. "Do what to Marco?"

"Nigga, don't play dumb wit me. I know yo brother killed him. My girl told me y'all tried to rob him and some mo shit."

"Ain't nobody rob nobody, yo girl a goddamn liar."

"Whateva. Hope you got bond money cause the streets talking like Grandma at Sunday service."

"Man, fuck the streets and fuck what you talkin bout. Neither one of y'all know shit," Gutta roared.

Ebony knew she should drop the subject. The look in his eyes always exposed his anger. That look made Ebony's pussy wetter than New Orleans after Hurricane Katrina. Knowing he would never turn down an opportunity to practice, she walked over to him. Aggressively she pushed him to the couch, straddling him like she was preparing for a bull ride. "Aww, I'm sorry, baby." Ebony planted wet kisses all over his face.

Gutta's anger subsided as the blood rushed to his member. He pushed Ebony back just enough to undo his belt and free his soldier, which was now standing at full attention. "Sorry ain't gone cut it this time, shorty. You gotta show me how sorry you is," Gutta said, playing like he was still upset.

"My pleasure, baby." Sliding off his lap, Ebony dropped to her knees, taking all eight inches of his dick in her mouth. The sensation of her tongue licking up and down his shaft sent him into pure ecstasy. "Damn, shorty." Gutta closed his eyes. Ebony increased her speed, bobbing up and down as if she was auditioning for the Karrine Stephens part in the next *Super Head* porn tape. She continued her act relentlessly for the next ten minutes, causing Gutta to release his load in her mouth.

Ebony was disgusted. She only had two rules during sex: Don't grab her hair and don't cum in her mouth. Gutta had a devilish grin on his face, knowing he intentionally broke her cardinal rule. She shot up and ran into the kitchen, spitting the semen in the sink. "Fuck you, Gutta!" She was already gulping down her second glass of water.

"That's what you get wit yo gossiping ass. Make me some sandwiches while you in there." Gutta laid his head back to relax for a second and reflect on the circumstances that he and his brother found themselves in. Their lives were spiraling out of control, and there seemed to be nothing he could do about it.

As he began to doze off, he was awakened by Ebony flopping down next to him. With her was a plate containing three turkey sandwiches and some Doritos chips. "Here you go, my love." Gutta grabbed the plate, almost devouring a sandwich in one bite. Ebony stared at him, infatuated with the way he chewed his food.

"Bae, can you get me a bag or something for the rest of this shit?"

Ebony jumped at Gutta's request. Running to the kitchen, she quickly returned with a clear Glad brand ziplock bag. Gutta deposited the rest of the food in it to take to his brother. When he finished, Ebony saw this as a perfect opportunity to get rewarded for the performance she put on earlier. She leaned back on the couch, spreading her legs to expose her cleanly shaven vagina. Using her two fingertips, she gently massaged her clitoris. Gutta eyed her seduction surreptitiously. Abruptly he jumped up, grabbed the bag, and hustled to the door. "Damn, shorty, I gotta get back to my brother," he announced without breaking his stride.

"Oh, you gone carry me like that?" Ebony was irate at his antics.

"Naw, I'll be back." Gutta exited, hysterical at the look on her face when she realized she had just got beat for the head.

"Fuck that nigga." Ebony shook her head, continuing to pleasure herself on her path to an orgasm.

* * *

Back at the house, Ms. Tina, Gotti and Gutta's mom, had come home, raising pure hell. Hearing about the murder her son committed earlier that day, she was livid. "If you think I'mma be housing some fugitives, you got another thing coming," she yelled at Gotti, irritated with the fact he wasn't paying her any attention. He continued to flip through channels, attempting to ignore her rants. "You hear me, boy? Look at me when I talk to you."

"Ma, I told you I ain't do shit."

"You a goddamn liar and you know it. Everybody heard them shots. It's only a matter of time before the police come kicking my shit in. Then what you gone say?" Ms. Tina had one hand on her hip, using her other hand to point her finger in Gotti's face.

"That I ain't do shit. Now watch out."

"Look, Gotti, I love you and your brother, but I can't stand back and watch y'all get locked up. So y'all gotta leave."

"Ma, that's some bullshit. You just ain't trynna lose your housing."

"That too, so either way you wanna look at it, you gotta go. I called your sister Tierra, and she said y'all can come stay with her."

"What! We don't know that girl. We ain't seen her since she left ten years ago. How you just expect us to move in wit a stranger?"

The conversation halted as the knob on the front door turned. Gutta entered, carrying a bag of food and smoking a cigarette. "Oh shit, Momma finally decided to come check on her kids," Gutta joked at the sight of his mother looking like she was fresh off a three-day crack-smoking binge. Tossing the sandwiches to Gotti, he headed to the kitchen for a glass of tap water. "What she talking bout, brah?"

"She kicking us out."

"You goddamn right I am," Ms. Tina interjected. "And you ain't gotta ask him like I ain't standing right here. Like I was saying, Tierra on her way to come get y'all, so pack up."

"Shiiiit, I'm outta here." Gutta quickly sprinted upstairs to pack what little things he had to take with him. He had been longing for a change in his life for some time now. Even though he really wasn't acquainted with his sister Tierra, he saw this as an opportunity of a lifetime.

As he threw his clothes in garbage bags, Gotti came upstairs and fell on the bed. "Wassup, bruh, why you not packing?" Gutta asked.

"Man, I ain't trynna go wit no Gucci. We don't even know that bitch." The look in Gotti's eyes told his brother the move was actually weighing on him. Gotti wasn't accustomed to change, and leaving the apartment he grew up in and the only hood he knew wasn't one he was trying to make.

"We gone be aight, though. And truth be told, you know we gotta leave for a lil bit. Shit hot out here for us right now." Gutta tried his best to erase Gotti's apprehension.

"I know, man. Shit just getting crazy right now."

"Look, I heard Gucci doing her thing. Plus I been waiting for the day when I can escape this hellhole and never come back. This might be our blessing in disguise."

Gotti contemplated the message his younger brother was relaying to him. In all reality he wanted to leave long before Gutta. Over time he just wound up accepting the fact that it may never happen. Warming up to the idea, Gotti sat up with a solemn expression. "Ay, Gutta."

"Yo."

"You gotta promise me something."

Gutta stopped packing to give Gotti his undivided attention. "Anything. Wassup?"

"Promise me we gone stay loyal to each other."

Gutta squinted his eyes, giving the look of confusion at his brother's request. "You already know that, my nigga."

"Real talk, tho, love and loyalty always."

"Dawg, I'mma foreva be my brother's keeper. That shit ain't neva gone change."

"Gotti! Gutta!"

The boys squenched at the sound of Ms. Tina screaming their names. They hated how high-pitched her voice got when she yelled. "What!" they both answered in unison.

"Come downstairs."

As the boys descended the staircase, they were in awe at the beauty of the girl standing in their living room. Tierra, aka Gucci, was a five-foot-nine-inch-tall redbone with an astonishing 33-24-44 figure. Add that with the red True Religion dress, black red-bottom heels, and Gucci shades she wore, and she would easily rival some of the baddest video vixens ever. "Damn" was all the brothers could manage to say as they reached the bottom of the steps.

Ms. Tina, knowing how far in the gutter her sons' minds were, decided to nip their dreams in the bud before they even got started. "Ain't no damn. Boys, this your sister." She put enphasis on the word *sister*.

"We know, Ma, we just ain't seen her in a while," Gotti said. "Wassup, sis?"

"Ain't shit. I heard y'all got in some trouble."

"Naw, people just trynna put our name in some dumb shit and Mama going for it."

"Already." Gucci admired her brothers for keeping it real with each other. The boys chuckled at her response, noticing how similar they were after being apart for so long. "So y'all coming with me or nah?"

"Don't seem like we got a choice."

"Aight, go get y'all shit." The brothers hustled upstairs and came back with two book bags and a trash bag full of hand-me-down-looking clothes. "That's it? That's all y'all stuff?"

"Yeah, why?"

Gucci shook her head with disappointment. She prided herself on her style and immaculate wardrobe of top-shelf fashion and designer clothing. Without saying another word, she spun on her heels, leaving the house with the door ajar for the boys to follow.

Before they could exit fully, they were stopped by the sound of their mother sobbing at the kitchen table. They gave each other a look of acknowledgment. Dropping their bags, they went into the kitchen to show Ms. Tina some love before they left. Standing over her, Gotti grabbed his mother's arm, lifting her up. "Give me a hug, Ma." Her tears flowed like the Panama Canal. She embraced both her sons, one arm around one and one around the other. There was nothing left to be said as the brothers broke the embrace. That day they walked out realizing their love for their mother had never wavered, regardless of her having them live like Third World slaves.

As the brothers stepped outside, they noticed the candy-apple-red Infiniti Q50 with Gucci sitting in the driver's seat. She popped the trunk as they approached the car so they could place their bags in. Looking at them through tinted shades, she said, "I don't know why y'all brung them raggedy ass clothes. We going shopping anyway."

"What you mean, shopping?" the boys asked.

"Yeah, shopping. Let me guess, y'all never been shopping before."

"Hell naw," Gotti, who was sitting in the front seat, responded.

Gucci could do nothing but grin. She was far too familiar with the lifestyle she had just rescued her brothers from. As she started the car up, the touchscreen TV popped out the dash and the system kicked in fully, displaying the twelve-inch speakers in the trunk. *All these bitches is my sons/and I ain't talking bout Phoenix/bitch I get money so I does what I pleases/I live where the muthafuckin pools and the trees is*, Nicki Minaj rapped as she threw the car in reverse and sped off, heading to Patrick Henry Mall.

Chapter 2

Ring…ring. "Yo."

"You have a collect call from Torn, an inmate at Beaumont juvenile detention center. To accept, please dial zero." *Beep!* "This call may be recorded and monitored. Thank you."

"Yo."

"What's good, Fatts?"

"Ain't shit, my nigga, I was waiting for you to call."

"Oh yeah? I called, so wassup?"

"I guess you ain't heard, hunh?"

"Heard what?"

There was an awkward silence before Fatts responded. "Man, some fucked-up shit happened this morning."

"Aight, what that gotta do wit me?"

"It's yo brother, my nigga, but don't even sweat it. You know I'mma ride for brah."

"Who, Marco? What happened to Marco?" There was more silence. "Fatts! Yo, stop beating around the fuckin bush. What happened to my brother, fam?"

"He… He got in some shit with Gotti and he shot him."

"Fuck you mean he shot him? Who shot who?"

"Gotti shot Marco, fam, he gone… Marco dead, my nigga."

Torn struggled to stay on his feet as he was weakened by the news. With a pain in his chest and tears in his eyes, he dropped the phone and stormed towards his cell, not wanting to break down in front of the other inmates. The moment he crossed the threshold, he fell backwards, sliding down the wall, unable to control the tears from streaming down his cheeks. He let out a gut-wrenching scream.

At the sight of his cell partner in so much pain, Noon jumped from the top bunk and kneeled in front of his heartsick friend. "Wassup, Torn? What happened, my nigga?" Noon questioned, concerned over what could have crippled his comrade so quickly.

Torn struggled to fight back his tears. "They… They killed him."

"Who, my nigga? Who got killed?"

"Marco. They killed my fucking brother, fam!"

"Damn" was all Noon could muster, knowing how close Torn was to his only sibling. There were no words that would be sufficient enough to console his friend. Aware of that, he decided the best course of action would be to leave and give Torn time to greive in peace. He slowly stood up and walked to his bunk. Grabbing the spliff he had rolled up under his mat, he passed it to Torn, offering one last sentiment before walking out. "Keep yo head up, my nigga."

Marco was more than just a brother to Torn. He was his father, idol, mentor, and best friend. The only one to step up when they lost their parents in a fatal car crash when he was just ten years old. Torn picked his head up and reached into his pocket. Retrieving his lighter, he sparked the spliff Noon handed him before he left. As he sat on the floor, eyes closed, smoking his problems away, he reflected back to the day his life was completely dismantled.

* * *

It was a cold December day and a youthful Torn was excited to be getting off the bus after a long day at school. He was exhausted from the day's activities but his brother waiting for him at the bus stop gave him the added adrenaline he needed to be his usual hyper self. He couldn't wait to be reunited with Marco, knowing a piggyback ride was a tradition whenever his brother picked him up. "Marcooo!" Torn yelled, leaping off the steps and right into his brother's arms.

"Hey, lil soldier, how yo day go?" Marco caught his brother, holding him in a long embrace.

"It was good. I got a green card today."

"Wow. I guess you want a piggyback ride, hunh?"

"Of course, Marco, you owe me one. I did good today." Marco put his finger on his chin, looking at the sky as if he was contemplating on whether to give his brother the ride or not. "Pleeeasse!" Torn had his hands interlocked, ready to start praying if he had to.

"Since you put it that way…" Marco swung Torn onto his back and spun around three times before galloping full speed towards their house.

The second they stepped through the doorway, Marco collapsed on the living room floor with Torn on top of him. They both were out of breath and laughing hysterically. "Where's Mom and Dad?" Torn asked as the laughter quieted. Both brothers sat up, noticing the house was silent.

"They should be here." Marco's head was on a swivel as he searched for any sign of movement. "Dad said they were on the way a hour ago."

"Mom! Dad!" the brothers called out but there was no answer.

"Well, by the time you do your homework and we eat up all the ice cream, they should be here, but you gotta hurry so we can clean up the evidence when we done."

"Yeaaa!" Torn yelled, jumping up to do his homework before his parents arrived.

Two hours and a whole tub of orange sherbert ice cream later, the boys sat at the kitchen table, rubbing their stomachs like the Pillsbury dough boy. "Wow, lil man, you ate more than me and I'm stuffed." Marco felt like he had just gained an extra ten pounds.

"Me too but I got room for candy."

"Nah, soldier, don't push your luck. Momma gone be here any minute to rain on our parade." Realizing it was turning dark outside and their parents still weren't home, Marco decided to ring his dad's cellphone. He dialed the number three times, reaching the same result. *I'm sorry, you have reached the voicemail box of Mr. Knight. Please leave a message after the tone.* Marco had to admit at this point he was becoming a little worried.

"What he say, Marco?" Torn had a suspicious look on his face.

Not wanting his little brother to sense his panic, Marco put on a forced smile. "He said if you not cleaned up by time he get here, you gone be in trouble," he answered, nudging his brother towards the back of the house.

Standing in the bathroom doorway while Torn cleaned his face, he suddenly heard somebody banging on the front door. Marco, with Torn right on his heels, dashed to answer. They both were optimistic it was their parents. The air was instantly sucked out of the room as Marco opened to the presence of two Arnold Schwarzenegger-looking police officers standing on the other side. "Are you Marcus Knight?"

Marco knew whenever the police were involved, it was never good, so before he answered, he turned to his little brother. "Go in your room, Torn."

Torn defiantly crossed his arms and scowled at Marco, attempting to hold his ground. "No, I'm trynna see too."

"I said Go!"

Torn, knowing he had no wins, ran down the hallway, only to come back and peek around the corner, curious at what the police could want with his brother.

When Marco saw that his little brother had exited the room, he turned back towards the officers. "Yeah, I'm Marcus."

The biggest of the officers spoke first. "Son, I think we should come in and have a seat."

"No, I think you should tell me why you standing at my door."

Both officers looked at each other before the biggest one spoke again. "Mr. Knight, there was an accident."

Marco's heart started to beat like a wild African with a pair of drums. "And?" He was anxious for the officer to get to the point.

"Your parents were involved in a deadly car crash. I'm sorry, but they didn't make it."

Marco froze. His mind went blank and his ears were flooded with what you would call white noise. He went into complete shock, fainting as his knees buckled.

The sight of Marco falling to the floor startled Torn. He shot out of the hallway with tears pouring down his cheeks. Kneeling down next to his brother's motionless body, he shook him vigorously. "Marco! ... Marco, wake up! ... Wake up, Marco!"

* * *

Tears flowed freely from Torn's eyes as he snapped out of his memory. Incarcerated at Beaumont juvenile detention center since he was fifteen, it was hard for him to fathom that he would never see his brother alive again. After receiving a juvenile life sentence for murder, he was due to be released in three more years for good behavior. He always dreamed that Marco would be there waiting to pick him up when that day arrived. The realization that it would never happen infuriated Torn.

As he lay on his bunk, smoking and staring into space, he made his brother a vow. One he would give his life to keep. "I promise you, Marco, I will have my revenge... A life for a life, my nigga. That's my word."

Chapter 3

Gotti woke up this morning feeling like Prince Akeem from the movie *Coming to America*. It had been a week since he and his brother had moved in with Gucci. The five-bedroom brick two-story house was located off of Harpersville Road in the residential neighborhood of Beach Lake Estates. It wasn't a mansion or anything but equipped with a driveway, two-car garage, and mini basketball court, it was far from the dirt-paved alleys of Marshall Courts. Gotti was in awe of the 52-inch flat-screen TV, wall-to-wall leather sectional, and gold-plated chandelier that made the spacious living room look like the centerfold for a *Better Living* magazine. The dining room also was laced with a 52-inch TV, glass six-seating table with Gucci plates and silverware sitting on Gucci placemats. Every room he walked in was better than the last. He had to admit his sister had expensive taste and impeccable style. He smiled at this thought as he lay in the queen-sized bed Gucci had set up for him to sleep in. This was the first time he had a room to himself. Though he loved his brother dearly, the serenity that came with being alone was a welcomed experience.

"Gotti!" Gucci called his name from the intercom system mounted on the wall in every room.

Jumping out of bed, he went to answer, holding the button down. "Yo."

"I was just seeing if you was up. When you ready, come downstairs so we can eat breakfast together before I leave."

"Aight." Gotti went to his dresser and pressed play on his state-of-the-art iPod player that rested on top. "I'm on fire/whole hood blazin/hustle game incredible/ice game amazing/look in the mirror," he rapped along with his favorite artist, Yo Gotti, as he jammed his way to the closet to pick out what he would wear for the day. Gucci had him rocking all the newest fashions. The day they spent at Patrick Henry Mall had been like nothing he could have envisioned. Gucci acted as if she had a black card, picking up shoes and clothes without even checking the tags. Gotti felt like new money as he put on a blue Aeropostale t-shirt, True Religion jeans, and a white pair of Adidas with the blue stripes. When he finished he went downstairs, hungry as ever and fully prepared to devour whatever Gucci had sitting on the table.

Stopping at the bottom of the stairs, he took the time to admire his little brother sitting at the dining room table. Gutta was laced in a white Polo V-neck t-shirt, Levi's 504 jeans, the newest LeBrons, and a Cleveland Cavaliers snap-back hat. Gotti could do nothing but smile as he sat there fresher than a dope boy at the BET Awards.

He approached the table, shocked to find Gucci's boyfriend sitting at one end with Gucci at the other. In the time he was there, he had only seen T-Money a handful of times. He was a skinny dude, about six feet tall, 170 pounds, with shoulder-length hair that he kept in cornrows. He was the typical hustler, always dressed in the nicest clothes, drove the best cars, and had the baddest chick on his arm. Gotti wasn't able to fully analyze Money yet, but on simple observation, he seemed cool. By the way he took care of Gucci and allowed her to move her brothers in a house that he paid for, he couldn't be that bad.

"Wassup, everybody?" Gotti greeted as he took his seat. His mouth was salivating at the sight of the Spanish omelet, turkey sausage links, and blueberry pancakes on the plate in front of him. He never thought any food could compare with what Golden Corral had to offer, but at that moment he would have to second-guess that assumption.

"I made it myself." Gucci was smiling at her brothers' reaction to her cooking.

"This shit look amazing."

The compliment inflated Gucci's ego. "Go ahead and eat."

Gotti grabbed the Gucci fork that lay on the table, cut a slice of the omelet, and placed it in his mouth, chewing slowly. His eyes got big as Chris Rock's as the food caused an explosion on his taste buds. Without hesitation he put his head down, consuming the rest of the omelet almost in a single bite, then he started on the pancakes. "Damn, slow down, nigga." Gucci's comment caused the entire table to erupt in laughter.

"My bad." Gotti's mouth was full of food.

"Look, I'm bout to go out for the day to handle my business." Gucci reached in her purse, handing Gotti a stack of cash containing $300 in twenty-dollar bills. "Y'all hold shit down while I'm gone."

"Aight."

Gucci walked over to Money, giving him a long kiss. He squeezed her butt like he was testing a grapefruit. After about two minutes of this intimate groping, she turned, put her Gucci sunshades over her eyes, and strolled out the front door.

The men sat there eating in silence for the next five minutes before Money spoke. "So Gucci tell me you a trill lil nigga." He leaned in with his elbows on the table.

Gotti gave Money a curious look before responding. "I am what God made me, my nigga."

"Oh yeah. Eventually we'll see who you really are."

"What's that 'posed to mean?" Gotti was beginning to get irritated with the conversation.

Money was staring directly in his eyes, peering into his soul. "I'm just saying a pit bull can only tuck his tail for so long."

Not really understanding what Money was hinting at, Gotti decided to change the subject. "Word. So how long you been wit Gucci?"

"Long enough, but fuck all that. Come on, y'all riding wit me."

"Bet." Gutta jumped at the chance to get out of the house for the day.

"You too, Gotti." Money got up and headed for the door.

"I was chilling but since my brother so fucking hype, I'll go."

The boys followed Money out the house, jumping into his cocaine-colored Range with the cream-colored seats and Asanti 20-inch rims. Soon as he started the truck, the Alpine state-of-the-art touchscreen popped out of the dash and the JBL twelve-inch speakers kicked in, blasting Fat Joe and Remy Ma's new single, "All the Way Up." The three bobbed their heads with the beat as Money hit the gas, speeding out of the driveway and down the street.

Fifteen minutes later the Range pulled into the parking lot of the rundown Midtown Motel. The infamous spot was notorious for being frequented by mostly crack and heroin addicts. Money parked on the back side and gave the boys a nod to follow as he hopped out, heading for room 128. Soon as they entered, he immediately locked the door and turned, facing them. "Look, I'm bout to meet this fat nigga here to serve him a brick. I want y'all to wait in the car and when you see me come out, go in and rob him for the work back."

Gotti, being somewhat green to the drug game, wasn't feeling that idea. "That don't make sense. Why would you wanna rob a nigga you serving?"

Money chuckled at the question. "That's information you don't need, my nigga. All you need to know is I got twenty-five hundred for y'all, and whatever else you get, you can keep."

Gutta, who was quiet a majority of the time, stepped up. "Damn right. That shit sound sweet, but we ain't got no guns."

Money turned to the dresser, pulling out two .380 Highpoints he had stashed there the day before. He handed one to each brother, along with two red bandanas. "Just wrap these over y'all face and you should be good."

Examining the gun, Gotti looked up at Money like he had stupid written on his forehead. "Yo, where the bullets at?"

"You don't need them. I don't want you to kill the nigga."

"Man, fuck naw. You trynna get us killed."

Money, amused at the young boy's reaction, couldn't help but laugh. "My nigga, listen, dude not gone be strapped."

"How you know that?"

"Cause I don't allow niggas to meet me with guns on them."

Gutta, sensing his older brother's skepticism, grabbed his arm, turning him so that they were face to face. "Yo, I know you don't trust this nigga, but I'm with you, bro. Let's get this bread." Gutta's eyes pleaded with Gotti, knowing that if his brother said no, then he had to go along with his decision.

After weighing his options, Gotti shook his head. Turning back to Money, he accepted the offer. "Aight, fuck it."

Money, pleased with the brothers' agreement of his plan, handed the keys to Gotti. "Here, go park three spaces down, and remember, when you see me come out, start walking up, cause it won't be long before he lock the door."

The brothers moved the car three spaces down and sat waiting for their time to shine. Thirty minutes later a silver Cadillac CTS pulled up, parking directly in front of room 128. The boys watched as a short, fat dude wearing a Five x tall t-shirt, old Rocawear jeans, and a pair of all-white Air Force Ones stepped out, nervously looking over his shoulder before knocking on the room door. After the third knock the door opened and the fat dude stepped in.

"Wassup, Bubba." Money extended his hand, greeting the overweight hustler with a handshake.

"Ain't shit, what's good wit you, dog."

"You already know, chasing the almighty dollar. Look, tho, you ready to do this? Cause I got shit to do."

Bubba reached into his waistband, pulling out a brown paper bag containing $25,000 in one-hundred-dollar bills, and tossed it to Money. Money pulled a stack out of the bag and inspected it before returning it and tucking it in his waistband. "You in the top dresser, bruh," he informed Bubba before walking out the room.

As soon as the door closed, Bub went to the dresser and pulled out the brick of cocaine wrapped in clear plastic wrap. Anxious to get his nose dirty, he wasted no time before pulling out his pocketknife and making a small incision in the plastic wrap. He stuck the knife in the brick, pulling out just enough white powder to stick up his nose and sniff. The rawness of the cocaine instantly numbed his body, causing him to close his eyes and lie back on the bed.

Suddenly there was a knock on the door, followed by a loud boom. The door was kicked in with two men entering, scarves over their faces and guns pointing in every direction. Before Bubba could open his eyes good, one of the men made it to the bed, pressing the barrel of the cold steel to his forehead. "Where the fuckin money?"

"What money? Money just left."

"Don't play wit me, bitch. Take these fucking jeans off," the mugger spoke viciously.

Before Bub could respond, the situation turned violent. Rapidly the bandit used the .380 like a Louisville Slugger, repeatedly connecting the solid chrome with his face. Bubba curled over with blood dripping, staining the filthy room carpet. In one swift motion his jeans were ripped from his body. Carrying the denim with him, the robber dashed out the door, his partner close behind, the brick of coke in hand.

Money sat in his truck listening to music with his Glock 20 resting on his lap. He was hoping the pair didn't fumble and let Bubba escape. If by chance that was to happen, he was fully prepared to put him in the dirt faster than Smith Brothers Funeral Home.

On cue the motel door opened. The brothers came out, jogging to the truck with adrenaline seeping out their pores. As they jumped in, Gutta, who was in the front seat, shouted, "Pull off!"

"Everything good?" Money was calm as the still sea.

"Yeah, we good, but he ain't."

"What you mean? You ain't even have no bullets!"

"This nigga Gotti turned to Rambo in there, pistol-whipping the fuck outta dude."

"Word." Money pulled out of the parking lot, tires screeching. Once he was a distance away, he looked up at the rearview mirror to find Gotti staring out the back window with a stoic expression on his face. He had been in the streets all his life and had met countless gangsters in that time. There was just something about Gotti he couldn't figure out. Being a gangster in his own right, fear wasn't something he was accustomed to, but people tend to fear what they don't understand.

As they rode down Jefferson Avenue, Money felt his iPhone vibrate in his lap. He cracked a devious smile and hit the answer key, putting the phone on surround sound throughout the Range. "Yo, wassup, Bubba?"

"Money, I just got robbed, dog."

"No bullshit?"

"No bullshit. Some niggas kicked in the door right after you left. They probably was looking for you."

"Good thing I won't there then, hunh." Money wasn't the least bit surprised by the victim's ignorance.

Bubba began sensing ice in Money's tone when he answered. "Yo, why you talking like you don't give a fuck?"

"Cause I don't. Matter of fact, don't call this number. See me when you see me."

Bubba was baffled by the response he was getting. "Yo, where all this coming from?"

"You know my nigga Arab, don't you?"

Bubba's heart dropped at the mention of Arab's name. "Oh, so that's what this about? You set me up."

"Bingo! Yeah, nigga, karma told me hold her down while she was on vacation."

"Man, I didn't even know that bread was counterfeit. I told Arab that."

"All thirteen thousand? Come on, fam, don't insult my intelligence. That'll make me second-guess letting you live."

"Oh, so it's like that? I see what it is."

"Like I said, don't call my phone, and see me when you see me." Money hit the end button and turned the music back up.

As he continued to drive, he noticed his fuel gauge said he was on half a tank. Never allowing his truck to get that low, he veered into the Speedy Mart on 19th and Jefferson, pulling up to the only available pump. As usual Speedy Mart was buzzing with all kinds of activity. Nickel-and-dime weed hustlers as well as DVD and CD sellers stood in front of the store, soliciting to any and every customer who walked up. Money hopped out of the Range, turning the engine off but leaving the music blasting as he bopped his way to the front door. As usual he stopped to speak with the DVD and CD hustler. "Wassup, Hustle Man."

"Wassup, boss man. I got them new releases and classics for you. Fuck wit me right quick." Hustle Man displayed his black CD case to Money.

"You always got something going on, don't you?"

"Damn right. You know me, rain, sleet, hail, snow, I'mma be out here getting that doe."

"Come on wit that old ass quote, fam." Money let out a light chuckle. He flipped through the book for about three minutes before settling on two CDs. "Yo, let me view this Future and this new Step Brothers *THREE* jaint."

"You stay copping that new shit, ain't it. Look, this what I'mma do for you. Get you another one and give me fifteen for the three."

"Nigga, you sell 'em for five dollars apiece anyway."

"Oh nah, I raised the prices last week, but I'mma give you the discount."

"Man, you ain't shit but I'mma get this Money Bag yo jaint too." Money reached in his pocket, pulling out a stack of hundreds, twenties, and fifties. Pulling off a twenty-dollar bill, he handed it to Hustle. "Keep the change, my nigga."

"Good look, Money. You gone always be my nigga even if you ain't have no figures."

Money shook his head and walked away, laughing at how silly Hustle was.

After paying for his gas, he headed back to the truck. He nodded his head at Gutta sitting in the truck, jamming to the music. As he plugged the gas nozzle in the tank, he noticed a black Crown Victoria creep in the gas station and stop on the other side of the parking lot with the engine still running. The Crown Vick had five percent tints, which were illegal in Virginia, so Money automatically suspected it was vice. They were always taking pictures, harassing him like they did to every black entrepreneur in the hood. Shaking his head, he stared directly at the car, letting them know that he could spot a cop a mile away.

As he gazed through the windshield, he noticed the black bald-head driver had the smug look of murder in his eyes. Confused by the look, he instinctively slid his hand to his waist, gripping the handle of his Glock. Without losing eye contact, he placed the nozzle back in its holder.

Suddenly the car came alive. The driver hit the gas, screeching to a halt directly in front of Money's Range. The back window came down and a chrome Beretta stuck out, sun bouncing off it like a new diamond ring. *Boom Boom Boom.* The Beretta rocked the gas station as bullets found homes in the side of the Range and anywhere else they could make an impact. *Boom Boom Boom Boom.* The parking lot was now in a full-blown panic. The last two bullets found their way into the chest of an innocent bystander who was parked behind the Range, pumping gas.

Money, not able to grab the door handle and hop in, crouched down, almost crawling to the back of the truck. There was a brief pause after the seventh shot. This allowed Money the opportunity to point his Glock around the truck, squeezing three shots into the Crown Vick, shattering its passenger side window while placing slugs in the side door panel. *Gla... Gla... Gla...* Money's gun screamed its name as he dumped three more into the Vick, striking the tire. As the air escaped, the driver saw this as his perfect chance to get the hell out of Dodge. Sparks flew from the busted tire as the car fishtailed its way out of the parking lot.

Money, not wanting the culprits to get away clean, came up busting shot after shot, shattering the car's back window. *Gla... Gla... Gla... Gla... Gla...* He was relentless in his pursuit until the car swerved around the corner and out of sight. "Bitch mufuckas." Money hopped back in the Range, pushing the gas pedal to the floor as he fled from the scene of the shootout. The car was silent as everybody engaged in their own thoughts.

Gutta and Gotti had dropped to the floor as slugs penetrated the Range. Gutta, never before being in a shootout, was understandably shaken, while his brother, on the other hand, was furious. Gotti's initial reaction when the shooting started was to grab the .380 he still had in his waistband and return fire until he remembered one important fact: he didn't have any bullets. He hated feeling helpless when someone was threatening his safety and the safety of the only person he loved more than himself. He sat quietly in the back seat, vowing to never again be a position where he wouldn't be able to protect his brother.

As the Range pulled up to Gucci's house, Money turned down the music. "Yo, y'all niggas good, right?"

"Shit, we alive so we good," Gutta responded.

"Aight. I gotta handle some shit but I'mma get wit y'all later." Money reached into his glove compartment, pulling out $2500 and handing it to Gutta. Joyfully he pocketed the cash and exited the truck with a Kool-Aid smile plastered on his face.

Gotti waited until his brother had closed the door before he spoke. "Money, we good this time, but that shit can't ever happen again. Feel me? That's my lil brother."

Money nodded in agreement, understanding exactly where Gotti was coming from.

As soon as he stepped out, Money threw the truck in drive, speeding down the block and out of sight.

Chapter 4

It had been three days since the gas station shooting, as the WAVY TV 10 news reporter called it. Every news station in Tidewater had covered the incident vigorously over the last couple days. The cops were scouring the entire city looking for the shooters, since the innocent bystander who got hit had succumbed to her injuries. Gotti had watched every broadcast, looking to see if any leads had been discovered and released. He actually started to feel sympathy for the eighteen-year-old Hampton University student but quickly shook it off. It was better her than him or his brother any day.

As he sat in the living room watching TV, he couldn't help but notice that Gucci had been sulking around the house for the last three days. Money had not been home since the shooting, leaving her periodic messages on the voicemail system letting her know he was good. Though she knew the lifestyle he lived, it did little to help her cope with the loneliness she felt whenever he pulled his disappearing acts.

Gotti made his way to the kitchen as Gucci was washing dishes. She was in her own world, not noticing he was there until he jumped on the kitchen counter. "Damn, boy, you scared the shit outta me!" she yelled, almost jumping out of her skin.

"My bad, sis. I was just making sure you was good."

"I'm always good. Why, what happened?"

"Come on, my nigga, you ain't gotta play that tough shit wit me. I see you walking round here all sad like Beyoncé died or some shit."

That little joke got Gucci to at least smile, which was all he wanted to do in the first place. "Boy, you stupid," she laughed. "Nah, you know I miss my man."

"Yeah, I know, but Money good. He a soldier."

"Please believe I know, but this being a hustler's wife or a gangster's girl shit ain't all it's cracked up to be."

"Word."

Just then they heard somebody outside blasting music like they were trying to throw a block party. Gucci, already knowing who it was, took off, shooting from the house like a stray bullet. Gotti jumped off the counter, thinking Gucci was going to snap on whoever was disturbing the peace. He laughed as he reached the front door to see Gucci almost inside the front seat of the Range, kissing Money like he had just come home from the Iraq war. Satisfied, he walked away, leaving the couple to reacquaint themselves as he headed to his brother's room.

Without bothering to knock, he walked in to find Gutta under the covers, talking on the phone. "Wassup, nigga, who you talking to?" Gotti asked. Finding himself a seat on the edge of the bed, he lit up a cigarette. Gutta gave his brother a look, letting him know he was in the way. Gotti got the hint but could care less about his attitude. "Nigga, I said who you talking to?"

Gutta pulled the phone away from his ear, placing his palm over the mouthpiece. "Goddamn, pops, I'm talking to Ebony."

"Oh yeah? Tell her you gone call her back. I need to holla at you."

Gutta shook his head before doing as his brother requested, ending the call. He then threw the covers back and sat next to Gotti on the edge of the bed. "Wassup, brah?" He gave Gotti his full attention.

"Money home." Gotti was looking his brother directly in the eyes, knowing he was about to ask the same question he had asked himself.

"Oh yeah? What he talkin bout?"

"Nothing, he still outside wit Gucci."

"You think he found that bread?"

"I don't know but we bout to find out. Come on."

The day of the robbery, while waiting for Money to exit the room, Gotti had come up with the idea to search Bub's Cadillac CTS. Gutta quickly hustled to the car, popping the trunk to find a brown paper bag containing almost $25,000. Tucking the bag under his shirt, he jogged back to the Range, ecstatic about the discovery. They both agreed to stash the bag in the trunk of the Range under the spare tire until they had completed their task. Their intention was to inform Money later, but coming so close to death had made the boys forget all about it. The bag only crossed Gotti's mind as Money rolled away, taking the stash with him.

The brothers went downstairs to find Money sitting on the living room sectional with Gucci snuggled in his lap like a baby. Sneaking out the front door, Gotti posted up in the doorway to be lookout while his brother checked for the bag. Swiftly Gutta lifted the trunk door, moving the spare tire to see the brown paper bag still in the same position they left it. He quickly retrieved the bag, closed the door, and jogged back to Gotti with the stash tucked under his shirt. "We good?" Gotti asked.

"Yeah, we good, let's go."

The pair went back in the house, heading straight upstairs to Gutta's room. Once inside, Gutta locked the door. He then pulled the bag from under his shirt and tossed it across the room to his brother. Gotti caught the bag, pulling out two stacks of cash, each containing about

$12,000 apiece. The money had not been touched. "It's all here, bruh." Gotti tossed one of the

stacks to Gutta.

"Damn right. I just knew that shit was gone."

"Either way, we keeping this between us."

"Why? He said we can keep whatever else we get anyway."

"So it ain't no need to tell then, right?"

"Whatever, but damn, I ain't never seen this much bread, let alone held it."

The brothers celebrated for hours with the stacks of cash. Suddenly they heard a light

knock on the room door. Gotti, grabbing the stacks, ran to the closet, placing the money in a

Timberland shoebox. "Yo," Gutta answered with one hand on the doorknob.

"It's me," the voice announced from the other side.

Gutta surveyed the room, making sure everything was put up before opening the door.

Money entered, smoking a Jamaican-size blunt of exotic ganja. Walking over to the bed, he

handed the blunt to Gutta before taking a seat. "Wassup?" he said, looking back and forth from

one brother to the other.

"Ain't shit, wassup wit you?" Gotti had his arms folded, standing in front of the closet.

"Chillin. Look, though, y'all get dressed. We riding out in an hour." Without waiting for

a response, Money exited the room, leaving the boys to change from the basketball shorts and

t-shirts they were wearing.

Soon as he walked out, Gutta looked to Gotti with a confused expression on his face.

"What up with that nigga?"

"I don't know, but get dressed and don't bring no bread wit you," Gotti said as he departed to go dress.

Forty-five minutes later the pair gathered downstairs to find Money already outside sitting in the driver's seat of a midnight-colored Infinti Q45. The brothers hopped in the car, with Gotti in the front smoking a Newport cigarette. "What's up, Money, where you get this from?" Gotti asked, referring to the new car.

"It's a fein whip." Money turned the volume up on the system before speeding out the driveway, heading towards Interstate 64. Swerving in and out of traffic, doing almost 90 miles per hour, the gang reached the exit reading *Airline Boulevard* in Portsmouth, Virginia. They pulled into the Magic City strip club parking lot, finding a spot directly across from a silver Cadillac CTS. Turning the car completely off, Money grabbed his phone, sending a text message. Looking in the rearview mirror, he spoke to Gutta in the back seat. "Yo, you see that black duffle bag on the floor back there? Grab it and open it up for me."

Gutta reached on the floor and retrieved the duffle bag. Unzipping it, he found two Glock nines, both equipped with 30-round extended clips. "Damn, these shits tough." The war-type weapons excited him. "What you want us to do wit these?"

"Check this, my lil bitch just told me that nigga Bubba in there all carefree like he chewing gum. We bout to moke his fat ass for that stunt he pulled the other day."

Gotti quickly processed the situation. Money had to have valid information that Bubba was responsible for the attempts on their lives at the gas station. That day was still fresh on his mind as well. He felt just as disrespected as Money and it wasn't even his beef. That being said, he couldn't wait to retaliate on whoever it was that put his and his brother's life in jeopardy.

Reaching over the back seat, he went in the black duffle bag, pulling out one of the Glocks. After popping the clip out to make sure it was loaded, he pushed it back in and cocked it, placing one in the head. "So what's the plan?" The look on his face let Money know he was ready to put in work.

"I just texted shorty and told her we was outside. She bout to pop the fire alarm so everybody gone have to leave. When he come out, it's on."

Money, Gotti, and Gutta sat in silence for the next fifteen minutes before the doors burst open and a sea of patrons poured into the parking lot. The club was packed with Portsmouth's night life as every hustler and whore in the city seemed to frequent the popular spot. Gotti was mesmerized by the barely covered strippers trotting out in high heels and G-strings. His lack of experience with the club life made it a struggle for him to focus on the task at hand. Shaking his head, he snapped back just in time to see Bubba, along with two rugged-looking individuals, exiting the club laughing and joking, oblivious to the danger they were facing. "Game time," Money said, noticing the targets at the same time.

Gotti and Gutta both gripped their pistols, waiting for the okay from Money to turn the parking lot into a shooting range. Money waited until the three individuals had fully cleared the club's doorway before he set it off. He hopped out just as Bubba and his goons were crossing the parking lot. Sending three shots in their direction, he struck the goon to the right of Bubba with two bullets landing in his chest and one in his head. The other two momentarily froze at the sight of their homeboy laid out on the pavement, thoughts halfway across the street behind him. Following suit, Gotti wasted no time before he hopped out, dropping to one knee. Rapidly he released three shots that barely missed his target's hairline.

Bubba's other goon recovered quickly, pulling his nine-millimeter, rapidly squeezing the trigger. The entire clip was emptied in the direction of his enemies. Money, Gotti, and Gutta squatted behind the Q45, waiting for an opportunity to return fire as the two remaining targets sent shot after shot in their direction. "Damn, these niggas ain't playing." Gotti was breathing heavily from the adrenaline pumping through his veins.

Money analyzed the situation before coming up with a plan to end the back-and-forth battle. "Look, Gotti, me and you gone hold their attention. Gutta, I want you to go around the other side of the parking lot and come up behind them. Soon as you get a shot, slay they ass."

"Bet." Gutta began ducking from car to car, making his way through the parking lot without being seen. Bubba and his goon continued to send shots, reloading clips from behind somebody's now bullet-riddled Nissan Maxima.

After clearing his second clip, the goon crouched behind the car to load his last one. Bubba and the assassins battled for their next body. After loading and cocking his pistol, he looked up to see Gutta about five feet in front of him, gun trained directly on his forehead. The goon had the look of a deer caught in headlights as Gutta released two slugs into his face, causing his head to bounce off the car, breaking its taillights.

Hearing the shots from behind, Bubba was too late, turning around as Gutta popped two more slugs. One hit his back shoulder, spinning him around, with the second landing in his rib cage, sending him crashing to the concrete. Bubba lay there, fading in and out of consciousness. The hot shells burned his insides. He slowly opened his eyes to three faces of death standing over him with guns held by their sides. "Damn, Money, I thought you was gone let me live," Bubba pleaded through labored breaths while gasping for air.

"That's before you sent a monkey to tame a guerrilla."

"What you mean, dog? I ain't send nobody. I let that shit go."

"Yeah, aight." Gotti had heard enough. Pointing his Glock at Bubba, he pulled the trigger, knocking his brains into the pavement.

Sirens could be heard in the distance as the trio hopped in the bullet-riddled Q45, fleeing the scene. Silently they all prayed the car wouldn't break down before they made their getaway.

Chapter 5

Money woke up this morning fully rejuvenated after a long night of smoking, drinking, and sex with Gucci. He rolled over to find he was alone in the king-sized bed they shared. Knowing Gucci, she had probably beat him up, hoping to have breakfast on the table by the time he arose. It had been over a week since the Magic City massacre. Money spent majority of that time laid up with Gucci or going to various restaurants, clubs, and movie theaters. After his most recent disappearing act, she had come down on him hard, constantly nagging and crying about how lonely she felt and how inconsiderate he was being.

Money was a hustler by every definition of the word. Growing up alone with nothing had trained him to put his money before anybody or anything else. Although he did have his fair share of interactions with the opposite sex, he never met a female that could take his focus off his pursuit of the almighty dollar bill. That was until his fateful encounter with Tierra "Gucci" Walker. As Money lay in bed, he reminisced on the night he was introduced to the woman of his dreams.

* * *

The weather was great and the night was young. An up-and-coming Money strolled into the Paradise strip club dressed in the latest Akademiks clothing. He and his team had spent the entire day on the block selling drugs and dodging cops. When someone came up with the idea to go out to relieve stress after a long day, he went along. As he walked through the door, bypassing the line and search that was mandatory for everybody else, the DJ showed him love by playing a song from Future, who had become his new favorite artist. *"My fingers they itchin/they itching for that paper/Riding round the city and I got that calculator/I'mma muthafuckin monster when it come to getting that paper."* The spotlight shined directly on the hustlers. "My main man Money in the house. I see you, baby," the DJ shouted over the music as he saluted the popular drug dealer.

Money made his way through the sea of people, only shaking hands with those he knew. As he entered the VIP section, a stampede of dancers raced through the club. Their intention was to be the first to have their rent paid by the team of ballers. Money let his soldiers decide who would be allowed in while he sat waiting for the bottles of Cîroc he ordered to be delivered. The patrons outside of the VIP were filled with envy as the room was packed with the sexiest dancers, all while reeking of the best exotic weed America had to offer.

Money sat discussing business with his right-hand man, Arab. His partners, Dyco and Q Banga, were being entertained by three black Chyna-looking strippers. "My nigga, we did that shit today, didn't we." Money exhaled a cloud of smoke from the exotic weed.

"Yeah, I know, but three birds in one day off the breakdown gotta be a block niggas record."

"Gotta be, but I think I got a plan to get us off that block shit and put us in a penthouse somewhere."

"What you talking bout, my nigga? You just said we was doing good."

"Yeah, we maintaining, but I ain't never satisfied with survival, fam."

Knowing Money already had his mind made up, Arab decided the best course of action would be to go along with whatever his partner had in mind. "So what we doing?"

"First I gotta holla at the plug and make sure he wit me. If he stamp it, we ain't pumping out River Walk no more. We takin ova that shit."

"How we gone do that wit Mizz and them out there?"

"Like Nino did on the Carter, my nigga…like Nino did."

Arab laughed at how devious his right hand was. "Nigga, you wild as shit. You on some movie shit."

"My life is a movie, fam. I thought you knew."

The duo continued plotting their takeover until Money glanced towards the entryway to see the baddest female in the city entering, carrying a platter containing three bottles of Cîroc and a basket of hot wings. He was amazed by Gucci as she walked up to him wearing a red finger-length miniskirt, Manolo Blahnik heels, and a white belly shirt with the word *Paradise* embroidered across the front. "Where y'all want these?" she asked. Money was speechless, unconsciously biting his bottom lip as he salivated over the angel standing in front of him. "Heellooo! I said where y'all want these?" Gucci repeated, irritated with the lack of response.

"My bad, shorty. Put it on the table for me." Money finally came to his senses. He shook his head as Gucci bent over to place the items on the table, exposing the entire bottom half of her buttocks. After placing the items in the designated spot, she tucked her platter under her arm, immediately heading for the exit. "Ay, waitress," Money called.

Stopping dead in her tracks, Gucci turned around, heading back to his section, pulling out her pen and notepad, prepared to take his order. "What's up? What you need?"

"Nah, I was just trynna see if you wanted a tip."

"I mean, if you gone give me one, I'll definitely take it."

"Come here, sit down wit me real quick."

"What?"

"That's the tip. You should come sit down wit me."

"Nigga, miss me wit that weak ass game. I ain't one of these groupie ass bitches trynna scheme on a come-up. I work for mine, so since you don't want shit, I'm going back to work," Gucci snapped before making her exit.

"Daaammn!" Dyco, Q, and Arab were weak, laughing at their homeboy for getting dissed by a female.

"Damn, you ain't neva seen how to be a player, hunh," Arab joked while play-punching Money in the arm.

"That's crazy." Money laughed along with his team, knowing he rarely gave them something to joke him about. He usually wasn't the type to chase any female, but he was completely smitten with the waitress and knew he just couldn't let her go without a fight. "Q Banga, go get that nigga Big Bill for me," he said, sending for the owner of the club.

Big Bill was a skinny, midnight-black dude about six feet tall but only weighing 150 pounds. Nobody knew why he called himself Big Bill, being as though he was the exact opposite of what his name insinuated. Big Bill was a retired pimp from the '90s who ended up in a federal prison after being convicted on prostitution and human trafficking charges. Since coming home he had completely abandoned the game, using the money he had stashed for a rainy day to open the Paradise strip club on Warwick Boulevard in Newport News, Va. Even though he had not pimped in years, he still carried himself like he was the new age Goldie from *The Mack* movie.

About ten minutes later Big Bill walked in, wearing an all-white linen outfit, button-down shirt and all. The tan Kangol cap he wore backwards matched perfectly with the tan Stacy Adam shoes he stepped in. Equipped with enough jewelry to make Jerome from the show *Martin* jealous, he could easily pass for the smoothest pimp in the city. "Money Man, what it do, baby?" Bill greeted nervously like he was walking up to Don Corleone.

Money stood up to embrace the OG with a dap-slash-hug, letting Bill know it was all love. "What it go for, unc?" Money threw his arm around the old head's shoulder.

"You know the pussy free but the game gone cost you, nephew." The room erupted in laughter at Bill's slick talk. Everybody who knew him had major respect for the old head. He had done his time in the game, the street, and the clink. See him today and you'll think he got off scot-free, as he told anybody with ears to listen.

"Sit down wit me for a sec." Money pointed to a spot next to the one he sat in. Bill quickly obliged, plopping down where directed. Money got down to business. "Listen, shorty that just brought us these bottles. Who is she?"

"Oh, you talking bout bougie ass Gucci. Nephew, I think the girl gay. She act like she ain't had no dick."

Money almost laughed at Bill's comment but remained serious so the old man wouldn't confuse his laughter with compromise. "I want you to give her the night off and get her to my section."

"How I'mma do that? Money, I'm telling you the girl got more issues than *Jet*. Don't sweat it, though, nephew. I got a bitch on my roster that'll make you think Gucci was nothing but a knockoff."

Money reached into his pocket, pulling out a stack of one-hundred-dollar bills. Peeling off three, he handed them to Big Bill. "I want her."

Bill looked down at the cash before he grabbed it, tucking it away in his top shirt pocket. "Nephew, she might be duct-taped, blindfolded, and gagged, but she gone be here, just you wait." Big Bill was adamant as he got up to retrieve the gorgeous waitress.

Gucci was in the kitchen area, preparing a tray for her next customers, when he ran into her. Grabbing her hand, he lifted it to his lips, planting a kiss on her soft skin. "Gucci, how you doing, baby girl?"

"I'm good, why? Why you acting like that?" Gucci had a confused look on her face while picking up her tray en route to her next destination. Big Bill snatched the tray from Gucci, almost sending the entire platter crashing to the floor. "What the fuck you doing?!" she snapped, catching the tray moments before it slipped from her grasp.

"Girl, you work too much anyway. How bout you take the night off and go have some drinks in the VIP?"

"I got bills to pay, Bill. I ain't got time to drink."

"Baby girl, you good. I'mma still pay you. You know Big Daddy Bill got you." Bill patted his chest like he was going to handle things.

Any other girl would have jumped at the chance to get the night off, but not Gucci. She saw right through Bill's lame excuse for game. "Nah, I'm good, Bill. You can't pay me to entertain some niggas like I'm Pinky or some shit."

Bill was tired of playing games with the hardheaded waitress. He didn't like having to ask any female anything more than once. "Either you going to that VIP room or the next drinks you carry gone be to the drive-thru at Wendy's. You choose."

Gucci wanted to snap on Bill for his lack of respect, but the truth is she really didn't have a leg to stand on. Her job was the only way she paid her rent every month, and she refused to go back to Marshall Courts with her cracked-out mother. Furious, Gucci stormed off towards the VIP, biting her tongue so hard she could taste blood in her mouth. Crossing the threshold, she marched directly to the table, snatching the entire bottle of Cîroc before flopping down in the spot next to Money. She paid him no attention as she took the bottle to her lips and threw her head back, swallowing a major gulp of the potent liquor.

"Damn, shorty, you ain't mad, is you?" Money admired how her eyebrows seemed to connect when she was upset.

"I can't stand that half-dead muthafucka. I don't get paid enough for this shit, word."

Money noticed Gucci was fighting back tears. "He gave you the night off with pay, didn't he? So why you mad?"

"It ain't what you do, it's how you do it. And as for you, that shit won't cool, sending that nothing ass nigga at me."

Money genuinely felt bad for causing Gucci the pain that was now evident in her voice. Extending his arm across the headrest behind her, he used his other hand to turn Gucci's face towards him. He made sure they locked eyes so she could see how sincere he was when he spoke. "That's my bad, shorty. I was being too thirsty so I gotta apologize for whatever disrespect you had to endure on my behalf. That being said, if it's alright with you, I would like to start over. My name Taurus but everybody call me T-Money."

"Well, my name Tierra but you can call me Gucci." She extended her hand to Money for him to kiss. From that day forward their future was sealed. The couple was pretty much inseparable.

* * *

Money couldn't control his smile as he thought on how his love had progressed. She had proven herself time and time again over the years. Though he had moments of infidelity, he vowed to never give loyalty to any female other than her.

He sat up as the door to the full-size bathroom located in the room swung open. Gucci stepped out, drying water out her hair with a towel, wearing a Mickey Mouse t-shirt and some boy shorts. "Damn, why you get up so early?" she pouted while standing in the doorway.

"You act like you ain't want a nigga to wake up or something."

"I didn't, not yet anyway. I was bout to make a bomb ass bacon, egg, and cheese sandwich. With raisin bread and everything." She walked over to Money and bent down to give him a good-morning kiss. Soon as she got close, he pulled her down playfully, kissing and sucking on her neck and ear. "Boy, let me go." Gucci pushed against his chest in an attempt to get up.

"Lay…down…wit me…for a second." Money spoke in between kisses.

"Nooo, I gotta go make breakfast for my brothers, and I know you hungry after last night."

"I'm hungry alright but I ain't trynna eat no sandwich."

"You a fuckin nympho, bae, word."

Money wasted no time on a response. He simply climbed on top of Gucci, separating her thighs with his nude body. Gucci embraced the intimacy, spreading her hips even wider, allowing Money all the access he needed. Her pussy was wet as Niagara Falls as Money grinded his body against hers, placing kisses from her neck to her lips. "Oh my God, baby, what you doin?" Gucci bit her bottom lip as Money descended from her neck to her chest, placing kisses along the way. Lifting her shirt up, he exposed her firm breasts and rock-hard nipples. She took it upon herself to assist him, pulling the shirt completely off, tossing it to the floor.

Money's member grew into a full erection at the sight of Gucci's shirtless body. He quickly indulged, taking her left breast into his mouth, softly licking and sucking her nipple. At the same time he massaged her flesh with his hand. Gucci was in pure ecstasy. Her breaths deepened and her eyes rolled into the back of her head. "Ssss…ooo." She could not control her moans as Money switched from one breast to the other, providing pleasure to both equally. He smiled as he looked up to see her eyes closed and her sucking on her bottom lip, on the verge of a premature orgasm. Not allowing her to get off so easy, he continued his journey, planting kisses down her stomach until he was eye level with her candy-flavored juice box.

Gucci lifted her bottom off the bed as Money snatched off her boy shorts, tossing them to the floor beside her t-shirt. Slowly he made his way back to her completely shaven cave. Gucci let out a seductive moan as Money stuck his two fingers deep inside her. Using his tongue, he fondled her swollen clit. "Oooo…shit, baby." Gucci's groans let Money know she was enjoying the attention. He increased his speed, flicking his tongue back and forth while using his fingers to find and slowly massage her G-spot. "Oh my God…Money, baby, I'm coming, damn," Gucci shouted, warning Money as she pushed his face away from her gushing pussy.

Money was on both knees, looking down on Gucci. Her eyes were closed as she attempted to catch her breath. "Damn, bae, you ain't tapping on me already, is you?" Before Gucci could respond, Money was on her, diving his dick deep into her pool like an Olympic swimmer.

"Aww shit… Aww shit… Daddy, fuck me…fuck this pussy." Gucci's moans turned into all-out screams, giving him the extra motivation he needed to increase his strokes. He pounded into her twat like a pit bull with his pink thing out. The smacking of their privates colliding echoed throughout the room. Money savagely continued his assault, drilling Gucci as hard as his thighs would allow. "Ooo, daddy, you got it… I love you so much." She was in tears as she felt another orgasm escaping her body. Her walls tightened on Money's soldier, causing him to stiffen. His tool pulsated as he shot his entire load into her oozing pleasure box. Completely out of breath, he collapsed on the bed beside her, sweating like a plantation slave working in July's heat.

It took the couple a full five minutes to compose themselves before Money reached over, grabbing his pack of Newport cigarettes from the nightstand. Taking one out the pack, he placed the cancer stick between his lips, lighting it and taking a long-overdue drag of the stress reliever. He looked over to Gucci. "Sooo what was you saying about bacon, eggs, and cheese?"

"Nigga, you funny. After that I might make Thanksgiving dinner."

Money smiled to himself, knowing he had succeeded in putting his sex game down.

Another five minutes later, Gucci jumped up, heading back to the bathroom she had emerged from earlier. "Where you going, shorty? The kitchen downstairs."

"The kitchen? Nigga, I'm going to the shower." She smiled as she slammed the bathroom door. Money heard the water turn on, so he decided to go downstairs for a cup of coffee to hold him over until Gucci could make breakfast.

While in the kitchen waiting for the coffee to brew, he looked out the window over the sink. He watched as Gotti and Gutta were in the backyard, playing an intense game of one-on-one basketball. The brothers were pushing and posting each other up like they were sworn rivals playing for an NBA championship. Intrigued by the intensity, Money poured himself a cup of coffee and headed to the backyard to catch the game up close and personal.

Gotti had the ball in his right hand, using his left to hold Gutta off while he backed him down, getting closer to the rim. Gutta felt like his older brother was trying to bully him. Aggressively he pushed him back in attempts to keep him out of the paint. "Nigga, stop fouling me!" Gotti shouted. He was frustrated with his brother's hacking defense.

"Shut up!"

"Aight, matter of fact..." Gotti, ready for the game to be over, spun off Gutta's body, stepping back to hit a fade-away jumper reminiscent of the famous Kobe Bryant "Game." Gutta was furious. Gotti walked off the court with his chest poked out like he was the baddest dude to ever dribble a basketball.

"I see you, young nigga," Money applauded as Gotti walked over to where he was standing sipping his coffee.

"All that nigga do is hack." Gotti wiped the sweat from his forehead with a hand towel he had set to the side.

"I feel you."

"Look, tho, I been meaning to holla at you bout some shit."

Gotti and Money had been standing side by side, watching Gutta on the court intensely practicing his basketball moves. The seriousness in Gotti's voice let Money know to turn and give him his full attention. "Wassup?"

"I ain't trynna be in your business or nothing, but I think we done enough to where I can just keep it a band wit you."

"You already know. Speak yo mind, gangsta."

"We trynna get some bread, fam." Money smiled at Gotti's request, staying silent while he continued. "I'm saying we'll start from the bottom or whateva, but I ain't going broke again for nobody."

Money took a sip from his coffee mug before he responded. "Go get your brother. We ride in an hour."

"Word." Gotti couldn't contain his glee as Money walked away, heading back to the house. He had practiced his approach for days and was ecstatic to know that it actually worked. That is, until Money stopped at the door, turning back to where Gotti was standing. "Ay, Gotti."

"Yo."

"Bring that twenty-five thousand you got wit you." The smile disappeared from his face as Money continued his stride, vanishing into the house.

Gotti was shocked at the revelation that Money knew about the cash. He pondered the situation for about two minutes before shrugging it off. "Yo, Gutta" His shouts stopped his brother in mid shot.

"Yo!"

"Get yo lil dirty ass in the shower, we leaving in a hour."

An hour later the brothers emerged outside to see Money sitting in the driver's seat of a black-on-black Mercedes Benz G55 truck on 20-inch AMG five-spoke rims. They were flabbergasted as they made their way down the driveway, hopping in the spacious SUV. "Damn, my nigga, this shit hard body." Gotti entered the front seat, admiring the lacquer-coated dashboard with built-in TV and navigation system.

"This shit ain't bout nothing," Money stated in an attempt to remain humble.

"Shit me, it ain't nothing," Gutta replied from the back seat. "Hold up, tho, this joint won't out here this morning. Where you keep pulling these fly ass whips from?"

Smiling, Money veered into the back seat to respond. "I'mma let you in on a lil secret. I keep all my cars parked in various driveways in the neighborhood. That way nobody can easily pinpoint where I lay my head."

Gotti was intrigued with the thought process behind the action. He knew it was only a matter of time before he acquired the thought process and luxury items that the game could provide. After all, his mission was to live the opposite of how he used to live. To do that he would have to get all the things he never had.

Before turning the music back up, Money looked to see if the boys had brought the money with them. Not seeing the bag, he posed the question. "Y'all got the money, right?"

Gutta pulled the paper bag from his waistband, holding it up for Money to see. "Let me ask you a question. How you know we had the money, and why you ain't take it out yo trunk?"

Money looked back and forth between the brothers before he answered. "It's my business to know what goes on around me. I don't sleep on nobody. The only thing that come during sleep is a dream, but that's a lesson you'll learn soon enough." The boys sat silent, processing the jewel that Money had dropped on them. Pulling his Versace shades from the sun visor and placing them over his eyes, Money turned the volume up and reversed out of the driveway, heading to his next destination.

After about ten minutes of driving, the Benz truck made a right off of Jefferson Avenue onto Bellwood Road before making a left into River Walk apartments. River Walk was a small apartment complex consisting of seventeen brick buildings placed within six parking lots. Each building had between two and four hallways, each containing four apartments apiece. The buildings were separated by breezeways that led to a mini playground in the center. Even though the projects weren't as popular as downtown Newport News, it was a gold mine for any hustler who wanted to use it as a stepping stone to elevate from a gram to a key. That was until Money decided he didn't want to share the wealth anymore.

* * *

It was a cool February evening when Money and his squad decided to put their takeover plan in motion. Money pulled into River Walk's back parking lot in a three-car caravan trailed by his six-man team of shooters. Almost every hustler who was a factor in the projects posted up in the breezeway waiting for their next sale when the goons approached. Chris, Nitty, Red, Taye, and Vega put on the fakest smiles they could muster as they greeted Money with extended hands.

"Wassup, fellas?" Money obliged all the hustlers by dapping them up.

"Wassup, Money? Y'all deep. Ain't it what y'all bout to hit the club or something?" Nitty nervously asked. He was rattled by the deadly scowls on the faces of Money's goons.

"Nah, fam. I actually came to holla at y'all." Red attempted to walk off, hoping to avoid the seemingly inevitable altercation. "Hold up, Red. I ain't gone be long, fam."

"Oh, I was just going to check on something, but it can wait. Wassup, my nigga?"

"I just want niggas to know after tonight, ain't no pumping out here unless you pumping for me."

The hustlers were dumbfounded by Money's brazenness. "What you mean, Money? We all eating out here together." Red's comment caused all Money's goons to grip their pistols, ready to fire at the first sign of aggression.

"I'm telling you now that shit dead. If I catch a nigga sell even a five-dollar rock of some bullshit, I'mma push his wig back faster than Donald Trump's in a hurricane." Money's tone let the group know his demands weren't up for negotiation.

Chris, who had been sniffing cocaine all day, was feeling himself a little too much. Stepping up, he pointed his finger in Money's direction when he spoke. "Nigga, I was pumping on this block when you was still coppin quarter ounces of hard. Who the fuck is you to come trynna take over some shit?"

Pop!! The entire group's souls nearly jumped out of their bodies as Dyco pulled his P226 SIG Sauer, popping one slug into Chris's forehead, peeling his cap off like a vintage Coke bottle.

"Anybody else got something on their mind? I'm sure we can help you get it off right quick," Money asked. He looked through the group, giving each one individual eye contact. The crew was silent, each one inwardly fearing for his life. "Aight. Since we got a understanding, hit me tomorrow so y'all can get the details on how shit bout to run out here." Money and his soldiers departed on that note, leaving the remaining hustlers to choose what fate they wanted for themselves.

Over the next week a few more examples had to be made until everybody got the picture. When the smoke cleared, Nitty, Vega, and Red had met the same demise as Chris. Taye was the last man standing to run everyday operations of the projects, along with the team that Money put in place.

* * *

Fast forward a year and a half, and Money had the complex moving like his personal pharmaceutical company. He had apartments in every building set up like an assembly line. There were apartments where the raw powder cocaine was stretched, half being cooked up and converted into hard rock, or crack, as it is commonly called. After that the contents were sent to another apartment, where the uncooked powder was bagged up into half and whole ounces, with the cooked rock being separated into eight balls, grams, dubs, and dimes. The sacks were then passed out amongst the dealers Money had set up in different apartments throughout the complex. The process was designed so that no money would be lost or turned away. Over the last year the scheme worked flawlessly.

Money stepped out of the Benz truck, trailed closely by the brothers as a young, dingy lookout kid who had just been on the phone greeted them. "Yo, wassup, Money."

"Wassup, Mel, everything good out here?"

"Yeah, my nigga, shit moving like the Amtrak do."

"What about twelve? They ain't running down on my block, is they?" Money asked, referring to the police who frequented high-drug areas.

"You know, the usual ride-throughs and mean mugs, but they ain't been on no stop-and-frisk type shit."

"That's aight. Where Taye at?"

"He in the second parking lot at the studio."

Money and the brothers headed through the cuts, passing the playground on their way to the studio. Gotti and Gutta couldn't believe how serene the complex appeared. There were kids playing, mothers lounging in kitchen chairs gossiping with each other, some people walking dogs, a group of pre-teens joking each other, and the occasional drug addict power-walking on his mission to the next fix. The odd thing was there wasn't a drug dealer in sight.

The trio entered the apartment studio to the sound of a Timberland Caliber original beat bassing throughout the building. Two massive speakers held their own residency against the wall. In the bathroom-slash-microphone booth was a young rapper by the name of Jazz-o laying a fire verse over the production. "*I got some guala gualas to pop ya/send you to our father/and go back to Guatemala.*" Money, Gotti, and Gutta listened, bobbing their heads as Jazz-o shredded the track, replacing it with punchlines and metaphors. This was Money's part-time hobby. He found three of Va's nicest MCs: Jazz-o, Thugga, and Stress. With the promise of stardom, he signed them to his label, T.O.R.N. records.

Taye emerged from the back room as the track finished. Rushing up to Money, he extended his hand. "Wassup, boss man!"

"Ain't shit, fam. What my young niggas doing in here?" Money was referring to his three artists.

"Man, they rippin track after track. Sooner or later we gone have mixtapes done on all of 'em."

Money cracked a smile. He was delighted with the good news. "That's aight, but check this. Let me holla at you outside right quick."

The pair walked outside followed by Gotti and Gutta. Stopping in front of the building, Money wrapped his arm around Taye's shoulder as he spoke into his ear. "Next time I catch one of these lookout boys on the phone when they supposed to be paying attention, we gone have a problem like a math student, feel me?"

Knowing Money wasn't the type to make idle threats, Taye quickly relented, saying whatever he had to say to soften the anger of his boss. "My bad, big homie, I got that shit. I'mma straighten all they ass out. Don't even sweat it, boss man."

"Don't got it, my nigga, get it. But anyway, what them numbers look like?"

"Shiiit, we gravy on that. Birds flying like a earthquake coming. We already pulled in seventy-five grand. We should clear a hundred by the weekend easy."

Turning around to the brothers, Money gave them a nod to walk up and join the conversation. "Taye, these my lil brothers, Gotti and Gutta. They stamped out here from now on." The brothers both stepped up, giving Taye dap. Playing the background, the group proceeded up the sidewalk. "I want you to take they bread and bring back two bricks for me. Alright, where the bag at?"

Gutta reached under his shirt, retrieved the paper bag, and handed it to Taye. "Bet. Just give me ten minutes and I'mma meet you at the truck." With that Taye hustled off in the opposite direction. Money, Gotti, and Gutta headed to the truck with Money stopping to hand a few kids ten-dollar bills.

Gotti sat in the front seat, thinking about the operation Money had just introduced him too. It was like nothing he could have imagined. Eager to learn, he turned the music down slightly, making sure Money could hear him. "Fam, I can't believe you actually took over a whole projects."

Money chuckled at Gotti's admiration. "This shit ain't nothing. I know dudes that took over whole cities."

"How you keep the residents from calling the people on you?"

"Fear and love, my nigga. To control somebody you must first make them love you for what you do for them. Then you make them fear what you could do to them. That's the same way people got the fear and love of God." Money stopped to make sure he had the full attention of his young protégés. "On a more worldly level, I make sure every resident out here wants for nothing. These are all based off your income apartments, so most of the residents were struggling before I came along. I pay everybody's bills and make sure they get whatever necessities they lack in. On the other hand, if they ain't wit it, I just evict them."

"What, like the landlord or something?"

"Yeah, just without the thirty-day notice. I just send niggas in to put they shit on the street."

"So you like the godfather of the hood, making people offers they can't refuse, hunh?" The analogy caused laughter throughout the car.

"Nah, my nigga, I'm more like Bumpy Johnson of the ghetto."

As Money was finishing his lesson, Taye approached the window, carrying a black bag on his shoulder. "It's all good," he said, tossing the bag in the car. Immediately he strolled off in the opposite direction he came, pretending to be talking on the phone.

Money passed the bag to Gutta in the back seat before pulling out of the parking lot, exiting the projects.

Chapter 6

It took months for Torn to cope with the loss of his brother before he could stomach being around the rowdy young inmates of Beaumont juvenile detention center. He had been completely isolated to his cell a majority of the time, only making himself accessible to his cell partner, Noon. Aware of the situation, the counselors of the facility were constantly calling him to their office or coming by to check on him. Even the snitches who were aware of his loss were using it as a reason to pass notes to the staff, saying he was going to kill himself. A lot of people knew of Torn's reputation as a killer and most respected him for it. Those who didn't respect it were usually intimidated by him, enticing them to find any reason to write him out of the pod.

Torn being himself just wanted to relax and get high, but fear always resonates in the hearts of the scared. He lay in his cell reading his favorite urban novel, *Word is Bond* by Gutta and Lucy, when he was interrupted by Noon rushing in to put on his basketball shorts and sneakers. "What's good, fam?" Torn asked, dropping his book to the side.

"Ain't shit. We bout to get gym rec. I'm betting these Virginia Beach niggas ten dollars a game."

"Oh yeah? Don't lose all yo shit, fam. That nigga B-zo play on some rondo type shit."

Noon frowned his face at Torn's comment. "Man, dude ain't bout shit. He can't score when a nigga playing D on him. Come show a nigga some love anyway. I know you tired of holding down the cell."

Torn had to admit he was becoming a little claustrophobic from sitting in the cell all day, plus he had read almost every book in the Dumb Hard book series. "Matter of fact, I'mma come out there today, but you better show out on that court." He sat on the edge of his bunk, putting his shoes on.

"You know I'mma put on for the cell, my nigga."

"Gym rec!" the CO shouted before popping the cell doors. Torn and the other inmates were walking down the hallway, hands clasped behind their backs. Suddenly an eerie feeling rushed through his body. He began questioning whether going to the gym was a good idea. Not able to turn around, he brushed it off as simple paranoia and went on to try his best at having a good time.

As he sat off to the side, he became captivated with the intensity of the game. Noon had just knocked down back-to-back three-pointers. That was until Devon invaded his personal space by inviting himself to have a seat on the bench beside him. "What's up, Torn?" Devon greeted, attempting to spark a conversation.

"Sup yo." Torn continued staring at the players on the court, hoping Devon would get the hint and go about his business.

Unfortunately for Torn, he continued. "Good seeing you out for once. I heard about Marco too. Even though I went to school wit Gotti, I ain't feeling that shit at all. Marco was big homie to a lot of niggas out the way."

Torn just shook his head, attempting to disregard anything Devon was talking about. Even though they were from the same city, he never liked the dude at all. Devon had ducked plenty of fights in his stint at Beaumont, and Torn couldn't respect that. Sucker free was one of his mottos, and to Torn he was a cold sucker.

As the homeboys sat watching the game, Devon babbling and Torn ignoring him, they noticed the basketball game was going from intense to aggravated aggression. "Ayo, why you keep fouling me?" B-zo shouted after going up for a lay-up and getting smacked across the head.

Noon grabbed the rebound after the missed shot, forcibly throwing it at B-zo's chest. "Nigga, pull yo skirt down."

"Yeah, aight." B-zo inbounded the ball to his teammate, only to get it back, ready for his one-on-one battle. Noon got in his best defensive stance. B-zo dribbled the ball left, crossing back right in an attempt to get him off balance. Noon slightly bit on the fake, allowing B-zo to shoot past him on the right, going in for another lay-up. Recovering quickly, Noon chased his opponent down as he jumped, meeting him in the air with a forearm to the back of his neck.

B-zo was fed up. Walking up to Noon, he threw a wild haymaker that caught him in the side of the head, sending him stumbling to the floor. Without hesitation Torn shot off the bench, running full speed at B-zo. Applying all his strength, he swung a right hook that sounded like a firecracker when it connected with the ball player's jaw. The force sent B-zo crashing to the hardwood floor.

Noon jumped up, imitating David Beckham, kicking the injured ball player directly in his face. Not able to recover, B-zo curled up in the fetal position. The two friends continued their assault, kicking and stomping him relentlessly, trying to inflict as much damage as possible. A legion of COs charged in to break up the beating.

After being handcuffed and nearly dragged to the isolation wing of Beaumont, Torn lay in his cell, staring up at the ceiling, reflecting on how chaotic his life had been the last couple of months. With two years remaining on his sentence, the last thing he needed was another infraction on his record. That was sure to push his release date back further than it already was. He was furious at Noon for putting him in that position. At the end of the day, Noon had shown him nothing but loyalty, and loyalty will always be rewarded.

An hour after being in the cell with no sheets or blankets, Torn went to the door. CO Hubbard was making her rounds. Lakeisha Hubbard was a 22-year-old, five-foot-tall, 120-pound, mocha-complected female with a body to make black Chyna squirm. Noticing Ms. Hubbard was about to leave the pod, Torn began beating on the door in attempts to get her attention. "Ms. Hubbard, Ms. Hubbard, come here right quick."

Hubbard rolled her eyes as she approached Torn's door. "Boy, what you want?"

Torn gave Hubbard a look like she must be crazy. "Boy? First of all, I ain't been a boy since I got off my mama nipple, so miss me wit that boy shit."

"Well, excuse me." Hubbard had one hand on her hip as a slight smile spread across her face.

"It's all good, shorty, but check this, where my sheets at? I been here for an hour already."

"Oh, that's why you called me over here, for some sheets?"

"Damn, what you wanted me to call you for?"

"You know how y'all niggas do. I thought you had something to show me." Hubbard had a devious smile on her face, letting Torn know exactly how she got down.

"Shit, we can do that too. If you wit it, I'm wit it, but you gotta go get my sheets and the phone first."

"Nigga, you act like you doing me a favor. You cute and all, but I ain't a lock to even come back."

Torn curled up his top lip. Hubbard's attempt at playing hard-to-get was futile. "Yeah, well, while you make yo decision, I'mma be here waiting for you."

Hubbard walked away, making her ass bounce like she was stepping on mini trampolines. Torn was mesmerized. Soon as she exited the pod, he immediately went into action, stripping down to his raw skin while placing the entire jar of Vaseline within arm's reach. Scooping a handful of the cool liquid, he slowly primed himself up, preparing for Hubbard's almost certain return.

Exactly three minutes later she reappeared, walking anxiously to Torn's door. His requested items were tucked under her left arm. Soon as she approached, he stroked his now solid member like he was perfecting the famous Michael Jackson dance move. She was fascinated by his muscular build. He looked directly at her facial expressions the entire time. Increasing his speed, he produced a loud smacking sound. Hubbard remained hypnotized by his movements. Her cavern was now dripping like a faucet as she massaged her swollen mound through her thin uniform pants. It took Torn all of three minutes to erupt, sending semen shooting like a shaken-up Pepsi can. "Damn, you nasty," Hubbard finally broke her trance on Torn's body, giving his face a little attention.

"You like it tho, hunh?" Torn stepped closer to the door. "Is you gone give me my shit or just hold it?" He was referring to the sheets and phone that still resided under Hubbard's arm.

"Oh, shit, my bad." She popped the slot, handing him the items.

"Shorty, let me get my shit together, but come back later and I'mma build wit you, aight?"

"You promise?"

"Yeah, I got you. I'mma need some company anyway."

She exited the pod, leaving Torn to handle whatever business he needed to handle.

Thirty minutes later he lay down to use the cordless phone after taking a bird bath and cleaning his cell. *Ring... Ring... Ring (pause) Ring... Ring.*

"Hello."

"You have a collect call from an inmate at Beaumont Juvenile Detention Center. To accept, please dial zero now." *Beep!* "This call may be recorded or monitored. Thank you."

"Hello!" the female voice on the other end greeted joyfully.

"Yo."

"Hey, brah! What type shit you been on? Why you ain't call me?"

"What you mean?"

"I ain't talk to you in months, Torn. You ain't even call to check on your niece when her daddy died. That's fucked up."

That statement sent Torn into a rage. "Miss me wit the bullshit, Ebony! What's this I hear about you fuckin wit the nigga responsible for my brother death?!"

Ebony froze at the question, remaining silent while contemplating a response.

"Yo, I know you fuckin hear me!"

"Torn, calm down, it ain't even like that. I was just fuckin the nigga. Plus Marco ain't been round here to even see his kids, and he was right down the street."

"It don't matter, shorty. You was supposed to be family. I got love for you and them kids. What happened to loyalty, my nigga? I wanted to break that gossiping ass nigga Devon face when he told me you was laid up wit dude."

"Regardless, you know you my brother. Plus I ain't seen Gutta since that shit happened."

"I'm telling you right now, Ebony. When I get out, shit going down. If you sleep in the kennel, you dying with the dog, my nigga. Straight up!" Torn disconnected the call, hanging up in Ebony's ear.

Devon had run his mouth nonstop in the gym, offering Torn more details about his brother's murder than he really needed. He was infuriated to learn that Marco was outside with guys he considered friends and nobody chose to intervene. That revelation increased his list of targets tremendously. Even Ebony had betrayed his brother, and he was the father of her youngest two kids. Torn forced back tears, thinking of how his brother must be rotating in his grave. The city was in for a rude awakening when he got released, and no one would be safe, not even Ebony.

Chapter 7

Gotti and Gutta had been formulating a plan to get rid of the drugs for the last few days. Neither brother had enough clientele to distribute the cocaine in a reasonable amount of time nor were they ignorant enough to think they could stand on any corner and peddle the entire package. Sitting at the kitchen table, the boys had just finished using the technique Money taught them to cook the powder, stretching it from 2,016 grams to 3,000 grams even.

After putting the drugs into separate size bales, Gotti sat back to run his plan by his younger brother. "Brah, I was thinking about throwing our team some weight so we can move this shit faster."

"Who you talking bout, niggas from the hood?"

"Yeah, but only the ones we fuck wit, like Lil Man, Tye, and M.A."

"Damn right, fam! I swear we hold our niggas so much they feel oppressed," Gutta said, extending his hand to dap Gotti up.

"I was thinking bout Lump and them Twenty-First niggas too though."

"What! Man, they got they own plug. Plus you know they beefin wit niggas from round the way."

"Fuck that shit, brah. We not inheriting niggas' beef. We gone get this bread and let the soldiers fight the war."

Gutta knew it was no need to contest when his brother had already made the decision for them. "I feel you. If you stamp it, then I'm wit it."

"Good. Now let's orchestrate this shit so we can get Money that other twenty-five asap."
Gutta pulled his Nextel and handed it to his brother. "Call before we go down there."

Gotti grabbed the phone and dialed Lil Man's number, getting an answer on the second
ring. "Yo."

"What's good, fam?"

"Who dis?"

"You already know, my nigga."

Lil Man became energized at the recognition of who had called his phone. "Gotti! Damn,
what's good, my dawg? Where you been at?"

"Laid low, my nigga. You know the hood got hot as Arizona after that Marco situation."

"Man, fuck dude. You know I'mma hold you down like a seat belt. That's real talk."

"Already, but check this, I'm bout to be downtown in bout a hour. Meet me at the store."

"I'm already there." Gotti ended the call and handed the phone back to Gutta.

"You ain't gone call Lump?"

"Nah, we just gone swing through there when we leave Man and them."

The brothers hopped in a cab, pulling up to Twenty-Eighth and Roanoke, where Lil
Man's family owned a small convenience store. Lil Man, Tye, and M.A. posted by the entrance.
The brothers were fired up as they approached their friends, greeting each one with a dap-slash-
hug. "What's good, fam? Look like y'all up out here." Gutta admired the crew's swagger.

"You know we trynna grind up on a fortune, my nigga. But why you walking round wit
that book bag like you Dora the Explorer or some shit?" Lil Man asked, bringing attention to the
school bag Gutta carried on his shoulder.

"Speaking of that, let's get off this hot ass corner. We can still go in the break room, can't we?"

"Yeah, come on." Lil Man escorted the gang through the store to the small lounge in the back. Present was a wooden circular fold-out table, a couch, and a bubble television that was used mostly for the Madden tournaments that would make the Vegas gambling commission sweat. Each individual took a seat around the table, joking each other and reminiscing on their past experiences.

"So how y'all eating out here?" Gotti asked, getting to the point of their visit.

"We eating, nigga. Why?" Lil Man responded.

"Cause I ran up on a plug, that's why."

"I know that ain't why you came down here. Sha throwing us zips for nine hundred. Yo plug ain't got enough juice to fuck wit that, my nigga."

Gotti chuckled. "How much bread you got on you right now?"

"Bout fifteen hundred. What, you trynna hold something?"

"Yeah, let me hold that fifteen and I'mma let you hold this big. Just straighten the other two thousand when you re-up."

M.A. gave Gotti a look of bewilderment. "My nigga, you just plugged dude for two hundred dollars. You expect us to believe you moving weight now? Cut the bullshit, fam."

Gotti bent down, grabbing the book bag off the floor. Reaching in, he retrieved a clear ziplock bag containing four-and-a-half ounces of off-white crack cocaine, tossing the package on the table for all to see. Lil Man urgently snatched the bag. "Dog, you can't just be throwing drugs on the table all willy-nilly and shit."

"My bad."

Lil Man held the work under the table, examining the urine-colored blocks. "This official tho?"

"Buzz Lightyear know that shit a rocket, fam."

Reaching in his pocket, Lil Man fetched a stack of bills folded with a tan rubber band holding them together and tossed it to Gotti.

"Shit, I got fifteen on me too." Tye pulled a knot containing $2,000 from his pocket, counted out $500 and passed the rest to Gotti.

"Y'all make sure that bread right and we rockin like a mechanical bull," Gotti said, passing Tye his four-and-a-half ounces.

"What's understood don't need to be explained, my nigga."

Following suit, M.A. reached in his pocket, passing $1,000 to Gotti. "I ain't even gone wail. I ain't got but a band for you. How you gone act?"

Tye dropped his head in disappointment. "Why you always fuckin the money up?"

M.A. smirked, reflecting on how he spent the cash. "You know Ant lost his job today."

"Nigga, what that gotta do wit that bread?"

"We start talking, going over all our problems, and you know how we do. We got highhh." The room erupted in laughs as M.A. quoted Smokey from the movie *Friday*. "For real, though, Fat Duck threw me some loud for the low, so I had to cop. What's up, y'all good?"

"Yeah, we good. Fuck that weed shit," Lil Man volunteered.

Tye looked at him like he had lost it. "Speak for yourself. Let me get a quarter of that shit."

The collection smoked and cracked on each other for another hour before Gotti decided it was time for him and his brother to make their exit. They moved around the table, embracing the group. "We love y'all niggas, man, real shit." The friends returned sentiments as the pair headed to their awaiting cab en route to their next destination.

* * *

The cab cruised down Jefferson Avenue, approaching the corner of Hampton Ave. where the local Food Tiger convenience store was located. The strip was bustling with activity. All walks of life populated the concrete sidewalk along the street. Lump, KT, and Hot Boy posted up, conversing with a group of virtuous females who would perform sexual favors for whoever could smoke with them for free.

Lump, who was six feet tall, brown-skinned, and wore his hat pulled almost over his eyes, puffed on a black and mild when the brothers departed the vehicle. Scrutinizing the cab, he squinted, attempting to verify who it was that had just arrived on his block.

"What's up, Lump! You out here thuggin and you let us get this close." Gotti greeted the trio with daps and hugs.

"Damn, what's up, brah? You know I'm blind as a bat with earmuffs. I was bout to pop yo ass till you said something."

"Stop it. Everybody know yo gun don't bark. Yo shit purr, nigga."

"Nah, my shit roar, fam."

Gutta used the lighthearted jabs as an opportunity to announce his presence. "What's good, Lump, KT, Hot Boy."

"What's up, Gutta." Lump was the only one to speak. The other 21st gangsters just nodded.

Gutta and Lump's neighborhoods had been enemies for as long as either of them could remember. The rival projects had even been in numerous shootouts with each other, sometimes rendering multiple casualties. Gotti and Lump remained friends since elementary school, ignoring the hate, while Gutta, on the other hand, would always favor the guys he hung with every day. The pack conversed while Gutta stood in the background, surveilling the block for any unexpected surprises.

"Gutta, what's up with that book bag? What, you on some Boston bomber shit?" Lump asked.

"Nah, this my laundry."

"Well, yo laundry gone have these faggot ass police stop and frisk all our ass."

"Let's get off this hot ass corner then. We look suspect as hell."

Lump, Gotti, and Gutta hiked their way to Lump's apartment. Harbor Homes was a group of brick row houses that extended from 21st to 14th Street. Murder, robberies, and drugs were an everyday occurrence, forcing the residents to become immune to the sounds of gunfire and sirens. A lot of the young adults grew up embracing the action, but not Lump. One of few against many, his goal was to save enough cash to escape the ghetto and knew promoting violence was equivalent to squatting where you eat. His mindset was exactly the trait that made him a perfect candidate to help Gotti obtain the level of success he had in his sights.

Arriving at the apartment Lump used as his operations home base, commonly known as a trap house, they were greeted by a caramel-complected, 4'11", 100-pound seductress wearing white coochie-cutter shorts and a wife-beater. "Damn, Lump, why you ain't tell me you was bringing all these extra niggas with you?" Brandi said.

"Chill out, yo, these my dawgs. Just get us some drinks right quick." Lump led his visitors to the kitchen, presenting a prerolled blunt of exotic weed from the ashtray as everybody took a seat at the wooden table.

Gutta's head was on a swivel, observing the futuristic furnishings of the project home. Game systems, flat-screen televisions, a surround-sound audio system, and security cameras were amongst the numerous items that made the apartment look like it belonged to the Jetsons. An enlarged Kush Kloud banner displaying a microphone with a marijuana leaf in the background was displayed proudly on the wall. The banner represented the rap label and street team Lump originated.

The trio reminisced on their school days over blunts and bottles for half an hour. "Let me get down to why I came out here, though." Gotti was ready to handle business.

"What's up, my nigga? Talk to me, I talk back."

"I see you doing yo thing out here, but I might got a golden ticket for you. What you moving, bout a deuce by now?"

"A deuce?!" Lump chuckled at Gotti's underestimation. "Double that and add some. I'm bout to re-up with a big right now."

"Bet. This what I'mma do for you then. I'mma sell you a big for thirty-five hundred and I'mma match you a big. Just give me the other thirty-five when you ready."

Lump looked at Gotti in disbelief. "My nigga, where you gone get nine ounces from?"

"That's the good thing, brah. I ain't gotta get it, I already got it." Gotti reached in his book bag for the two packages containing four-and-a-half ounces of crack apiece.

Lump's eyes popped like Wile E. Coyote. "Damn, you hit a boss lick, didn't you."

"Nah, fam, right now I *am* the lick."

Lump noticed the fire in Gotti's eyes as he spoke. He had finally grasped the concept of money by any means, which was the kush kloud motto. Being a true friend since day one, Lump filled with pride, noticing the man Gotti was evolving into. "They say when one life is lost, another is gained. If Marco's death is what it took for you to finally live, my nigga, then so be it. Just don't waste yo opportunity."

"I ain't never going back to that life, dawg. I choose death over poverty any day." Gotti sat back, smoking the blunt of loud, while Lump went upstairs, reappearing with the $3,500 to pay for the product. "Good look." Gotti dropped the cash in his book bag.

"If everything straight, I should be hitting you up in a couple weeks."

"Already then."

The brothers stood to leave before they got caught up in another conversation. "Take yo time out there." Lump closed and locked the door behind them.

Gotti paused on the apartment's stoop to light a cigarette before continuing on his journey. His friend's advice resonated in his mind as he fished in his pocket for a lighter. He never looked at the situation the way Lump had. Marco's death had actually been a blessing in disguise for him and Gutta. It put them in position to meet Money, who introduced them to a life the drug game could provide. They had been shopping, slept in plush beds, and ate three full-course meals every day since being evicted by their mother. Unfortunately for Marco, his blood had been the down payment to their new life.

Boom. Boom. Boom. The thundering sounds of gunfire grabbed Gotti from his thoughts. Dropping to the ground, his heart began pounding like a Samurai on a Japanese gong as slugs whizzed past his face, knocking life-size chunks from the brick wall to his rear. Unable to find shelter in the open area, the brothers scrambled to get out of the shooters' scopes, retreating between the buildings. Hurriedly they veered the nearest corner as the shots continued.

Boom… Boom… Boom… Tat–tat–tat–tat-tat. Glancing behind him, Gutta caught a glimpse of Lump bursting through the trap house door, sending rapid fire from his Tec-9 towards the unknown assassins. Slowing their run into a power walk, they emerged on Jefferson Avenue, heading away from the gunfire.

"Who the fuck was that?" Gotti was still hype from the attempt on his life.

"I don't know but Lump let his ass have it with that Tec."

"We gotta get some wheels, brah. We can't be on feet dirty with no heat on us. We asking to be vics like this."

"I was thinking the same shit. We got seventy-five hundred. I know we can get on with that."

"Call Money and see if he know something."

Gutta pulled his phone and dialed Money's number. "Yo," the phone was answered on the second ring.

"What up, Money."

"Ain't shit right now. What's good?"

"We downtown on foot. Come scoop us right quick."

"Aight. Meet me at the McDonald's on two-six in bout fifteen minutes."

"Bet."

The brothers continued their journey until they reached the fast food restaurant.

Approaching the register, Gotti was instantly smitten by the chocolate goddess waiting to take

their order. Her Hershey complexion and petite frame was enough to make him salivate from the

door. Turning on the charm, he spoke. "What's up, beautiful? How you doing?"

"I'm good, how bout you?"

"Better now that I met you." The cashier lit up. Gotti continued, "What's yo name,

shorty?"

Mia extended the tag on her shirt displaying her name. "At least I know you was lookin at

my face and not my body."

"Um, I don't mean no harm but you ain't really got no ass."

Mia's mouth dropped. "Uh."

Gotti laughed heartily at Mia's expression. "I'm fuckin wit you, shorty. I just wanted to

see if I could get you to smile even brighter."

"Whateva, nigga. What you trynna eat?"

"Let me get two Big Mac combos with sweet teas."

Mia typed in Gotti's order, coming up with a total of $8.75. Reaching in his pocket, Gotti

pulled out five one-hundred-dollar bills, handing one to Mia before walking away. "Scuse me,

you gotta get yo change."

"Hold it for me, I'll get it from you later."

The duo was devouring their food when a mystic white Mercedes SLS convertible AMG steered into the parking lot, Meek Mills' "I Been That Nigga" bassing from the speakers. Astonishment was evident on the brothers' faces as the driver's door spread like the wings on a bald eagle. Money emerged from the vehicle, dressed in an all-black Balmain outfit, stepping in a pair of all-black Yeezy sneakers. The restaurant's patrons were starstruck when Money entered, taking a seat in the booth beside Gotti. "What's up?" He removed his Ray-Ban sunshades.

"My nigga, what the fuck is that?" Gotti asked, referring to the foreign car.

"Oh, that's just one of my toys."

"Word. You gotta put us in a whip, dawg. We out here walking wit a brick of work, and somebody shooting at us like they duck hunting and we the ducks."

"Shooting at you! Who shooting at you?"

"We don't even know. Shit ain't safe downtown anyway. What's up wit a hoop ride, fam?"

"A hoop ride!" Money chuckled. "My nigga, I'm T-Money. Come on, we out."

The Mercedes cruised Jefferson Ave with the top down, pulling in the parking lot of VWK car dealership. The lot was a fairly modest business, displaying used Caprices, Hondas, Infinitis, and the occasional Range Rover or Lexus. The owner's sister, a chunky brown-skinned New York native named Bridgette, or Q.B. for short, appeared from the shop, elated that Money had blessed her with his presence. "Let me holla at her right quick."

Money strutted over to the jubilant saleswoman while the brothers patrolled the lot. "What's up, gorgeous." Money wrapped his arms around her thick waist.

"Don't gorgeous me, son. Why you don't answer my calls no more?" Q.B. spoke in a heavy accent.

"What I told you bout that 'son' shit?"

"Well, why you keep playing me like that?"

"Yo, ain't nobody playing you, shorty. Don't act like you green or some shit. You know I got a wife and I been good on pussy, so answer for what?"

"That's fucked up, Money. Why I can't be yo wife? You know I'll do anything for you, so why not me?"

"Not right now, Bridgette. Let's talk about that shit later. Right now I need you to come through for me. Come on."

The pair walked to where the brothers were looking through the window of a gold 2005 Honda Accord. "What's up, y'all find something?"

"We was looking at this jaint right here."

"This Honda?" Money wiped his finger over the car's hood.

"Yeah, we only got eight grand, we can't cop nothing crazy."

"How y'all feel about that Lexus LS 430?" Q.B. pointed to the luxury vehicle across the lot.

"I mean, that shit fresh, but we ain't got fifteen thousand to drop on no car," Gotti said.

Q.B. nodded her head in Money's direction. "If he'll spend one night wit me, I can give it to you for six."

"You gone give it to them for six anyway, and I'll think about giving you a few minutes." Q.B. rolled her eyes and stormed off to fetch the tags. "Stupid ass bitch. Come on, let me show y'all something right quick."

Money led his protégés through a wooden privacy fence. The second half of the dealership contained a slew of foreign and luxury vehicles. The brothers were flabbergasted. They patrolled the lot, inspecting the Bentleys, Ferraris, and Lamborghinis. After reading the description tags on a few windows, Money led them back to the front. "I showed y'all those whips for a reason."

His words piqued Gotti's interest. "What's the reason?"

"Cause, like you, I never had nobody show me luxury shit like this, so naturally I never dreamed that I could attain it. I didn't think a nigga from the hood could be worth it. That thinking is just us oppressing ourselves. That's what I don't want y'all to do. Never be satisfied with a Lexus when other people driving Rolls Royces and Bentleys. You can always do better. You can always *be* better. You just gotta know what better is and go for it."

The brothers were immersed in the lecture when Q.B. appeared with the Lexus keys and 30-day tags. After putting the plates on, they drove from the lot, feeling like LeBron James after winning Cleveland a championship.

Money's words continued to reverberate in Gotti's mind. There was a point in his life where he was satisfied with living in the hood. He never felt something so exquisite would ever be accessible to him. The reality was anything he wanted to achieve was right at his fingertips. All he had to do was grab it. The flame was lit the day he pulled the trigger on Marco. Today that fire blazed like a phoenix born from the ashes. There was no turning back for him. Like Money

said: Why be good when you can be great?

Chapter 8

I'ma ride for my nigga/Die for my nigga/Get high wit my nigga/Flip pies wit my nigga/till my body get hard/soul touch the sky/Till my number get called and God close my eyes/I'ma ride. Beanie Sigel bassed from the speakers of Fatts' all-black Denali as he sat outside Sussex One state prison. Torn had been transferred to the adult institution on his eighteenth birthday because of his age and violent history. Today was his day to be released. Fatts hadn't seen his right hand in five years. Deep into his second hour of waiting, he was ready to leave and try again in another five. The plan was to spend the entire day with the freed jailbird, helping him to get reacquainted with a vicious society. He knew the loss of Marco would weigh heavily on the brother's mind. Over the years they had spoken numerous times on Torn's plan upon release. The answer started the same every time, with Marco picking him up. That was until the fallen soldier's life was snatched so swiftly. Fatts planned to try his best at filling Marco's shoes, even though he knew it would be a frivolous effort.

It took another half an hour for the gates of the prison to part. Torn walked out, wearing a tan khaki suit, carrying a transparent bag of his belongings swung over his shoulder. He stood on the curb, surveying the parking lot for any familiar faces, when he heard a horn honk in the distance. Acknowledging the Denali, he strolled over to the truck, tossing his bag in the back passenger side before hopping in the front.

Fatts extended his hand to Torn as the door closed. "What's up?"

"Ain't shit, what's good wit you?" Torn gave Fatts a firm dap.

"You free, my nigga. How you feeling?"

Torn pondered the question deeply. "To be honest, it's kinda bittersweet, my nigga. I mean I'm glad to be out that concentration camp, but I don't even know if I wanna be out here without bruh."

"I feel you, but check this. Grab that shit out the glove box for me." Torn opened the glove box to find a Glock 19 sitting on top of an envelope containing $5,000. "That's you, my nigga. Hold on to that right quick."

Torn extended his hand to Fatts for another dap. The loyalty of his homie was just what he needed to boost his spirits. "That's a good look, my nigga."

"You may have lost yo blood brother, but as long as I'm breathing, you gone always have one from another, feel me?"

Torn's heart warmed at those powerful words. Fatts was right; brothers don't only come in the form of family, rather loyalty. If you can count on them to be there when you need them most, that's worth more than blood alone. At the end of the day, love is love, loyalty is everything.

Torn thought to himself for a second. Searching on both sides, he pulled the lever, reclining his seat. "Get me off this plantation, fam."

"Where you wanna go, to the mall or some shit?"

"Fuck nah, I'm trynna get some pussy."

With that Fatts turned the key, roaring the beast of a vehicle to life. Turning the music up, he sped from the parking lot. *Till my body get hard/till my soul touch the sky/till my number get called and God shut my eyes, I'mma ride.*

* * *

"Happy, happy birthday! Happy, happy birthday!" The staff at Olive Garden sang as they marched in, carrying a three-layer cake decorated with Gotti's initials. Today was his twentieth birthday. Gucci decided she wanted to go on a group date to celebrate.

"Come on, man, y'all know I ain't wit all these surprises."

"Boy boo, stop acting like you too gangster to be happy. Just make a wish and blow the fucking candles." Gucci was not having any of Gotti's attitude. She went out her way to make sure everything was perfect, and she was not about to let him ruin it.

Gotti closed his eyes, saying a silent prayer before blowing out his candles. The entire establishment united in applause. The spectacle made Gotti's table the center of attention. "See, y'all got strangers all in our business and shit."

"Bae, you betta stop acting like that fore you miss out on yo birthday gift tonight," Mia whispered seductively in Gotti's ear.

"Shorty, you know all you do is show up and I give you the gift."

"Whateva. Just cause it's yo birthday don't mean you a lock for some this pussy."

"I ain't tripping, shorty. I done been up in there more than Playtex."

The other couples laughed at Mia and Gotti's unorthodox display of affection. A couple months after meeting Mia at the 26th Street McDonald's, Gotti had finally decided to go back for his change. Her admiration was evident when he entered dressed head to toe in Versace clothing. In one hand he held a bouquet of red roses, in the other was a pair of Balenciaga red-bottom heels. Her heart literally melted when he handed them to her, calling her his ghetto Cinderella. The frog had turned into a prince and was looking for his Sleeping Beauty. From that day forward, the two had become a permanent fixture in the dating scene. He molded her into becoming the exact woman he needed her to be. Time and time again her patience was tested. Through the countless all-nighters and brief jail stints, she proved herself by remaining loyal, honest, and true. Her faithfulness had earned her the title of being Gotti's wifey.

Tired of the couple's bickering, Gucci stood, raising her shot of Cîroc to propose a toast. "Listen up, y'all." She tapped her fork against her glass. "I just want to toast to my two beautiful brothers. You don't know how many nights I cried myself to sleep, hating how I left y'all to endure what I knew y'all would have to. When Mama called me to come get y'all, it was like the heavens opened and God granted me a second chance. I called myself being y'all savior, but actually it was you who saved me. Real shit, y'all saved me from a lifetime of tears and regrets, and for that I truly thank you. Looking at the men you have become makes me the proudest sister ever. The sacrifices you made for each other can only be rivaled by Jesus himself. You held each other down from day one, and now it's my turn. I promise you guys from now until forever, I will always remain my brothers' keeper. And to you, Gotti, happy birthday." The participants saluted with their glasses before downing the potent intoxicant. Gucci wiped tears from her eyes as she retook her seat.

Ebony, who was hugged up with Gutta, was overcome with emotion. Water sprayed from her eyes like garden sprinklers. "Damn, shorty, why you crying like that?" Gutta wiped the tears from her cheeks.

"Shut up, you know I'mma water head."

The party chatted and laughed for another 30 minutes before it was time to go. They all decided they would reconvene at Gotti's house for a nightcap.

Money rose, pulling a stack from his pocket to pay the bill. "Nah, I got it." Gucci stopped him, reaching in her purse for her American Express credit card.

"Stop playing, Gucci."

"Nah, bae, this my gift. Let me pay for it."

"Aight, Ms. Independent."

The fellas headed to their separate cars, each escorted by their significant other.

Gutta had one hand draped around Ebony's shoulder. His other hand was used to hold his iPhone to his ear. Halfway across the parking lot, Ebony was paralyzed with fear. "Ebony, what's up?" Her terror alarmed Gutta.

He followed her stare until his eyes landed on two thuggish individuals moving briskly towards them. They had guns aimed like members of SEAL Team Six. Before he could react, the thugs pulled their triggers, releasing a barrage of bullets upon any living organism in their cross hairs. *Bok… Bok… Bok…* Gutta, Gotti, and Money dropped to the ground, scrambling on all fours like they were performing a football drill. *Bok… Bok… Bok…* The shooters continued to send slugs, wreaking havoc on the entire business section of Mercury Boulevard.

Money was the first to reach his vehicle, reaching in the tire well for his Glock. He popped up, recklessly firing in the direction of the shooters. Gotti was next, also pulling a Glock from his tire well, joining Money in his pursuit of human life. *Gla… Gla… Gla… Gla.*

Feeling the mounting pressure of bullets whizzing past their faces, the shooters decided to retreat. They raced back to the Denali, hopping in with their heads ducked. Bringing the truck to life, they swerved out of the parking lot, attempting to make a clean escape.

Gutta, who was pinned down during the entire shootout, was livid. Quickly he darted into the street, passionately sending shots at the fleeing Denali. The busy intersection was motionless. The cars behind him halted as not to drive into the line of fire, while the cars in his path increased speeds in attempts to flee the range of bullets.

Relenting on his efforts, Gutta jogged back to the Olive Garden parking lot. His heart rate dramatically increased when he saw Ebony laid on the cold concrete, blood pouring from her neck like fuel from a gas nozzle. Devastated, he kneeled next to his lifelong muse. Using his palm, he compressed the gaping hole in her throat. Money, Gucci, and Mia ran to Ebony's side, also kneeling beside her body. They wanted to find any way they could help. "Yo, call the ambulance," Gutta screamed, urging everybody to search for their cellphones.

"Nah, fuck that. They gone take too long. We gone drive her ourselves." Gotti took off, returning within minutes in his cocaine-colored Bentley Azure. Money and Gutta lifted Ebony into the back seat with Gutta continuing to apply pressure to Ebony's wound. Money rode shotgun as Gotti sped away from the scene, going zero to sixty in a minute flat. Gucci and Mia each followed, Gucci in Money's Rolls Royce, Mia in Gutta's Porsche 911.

"Yo, she still breathing, right?" Gotti asked while swerving in and out of traffic.

"Yeah, she good. She gone be alright." Gutta was being optimistic as he watched the life drain from Ebony's eyes. "You gone be aight, bae, just stay strong. I love you too much to lose you."

Minutes later the Bentley pulled to a screeching halt outside the Sentara hospital's emergency entrance. Gotti was the first to hop out, sprinting through the double doors in search for assistance. Within moments the car was engulfed by nurses directing Gutta and Money to place Ebony on the gurney. Gutta's heart ached as his love was wheeled away, headed to whatever fate God had in store for her.

* * *

"Yo, why you shoot the bitch? I know yo aim ain't that rusty. You had Gutta right there," Fatts questioned Torn's motives as they headed to his baby mother's house in the Fox Hill section of Hampton. They had been cruising up Mercury when he noticed Gotti's car parked in the Olive Garden parking lot. Abruptly pulling in, he pointed the car out to Torn, knowing exactly how his partner in crime wanted to address the situation. The taste of revenge was on the tip of Torn's tongue as he patiently waited for his brother's murderers to reveal their faces. He was in utter disbelief when Gutta walked out escorted by his brother's baby mother. He felt nothing short of hate as he hopped out with the full intention of separating Ebony's $50 weave from her scalp.

"Come on, dawg, you know I got aim like the toothpaste. I meant to push that disloyal ass bitch wig back. I wanted Gutta to watch her body drop just like he watched my brother drop."

Fatts was impressed. "Damn, you cold as ice, my nigga. That's yo brother baby mama."

"I don't give a fuck, fam. I'm telling you these niggas gone feel my pain. I'mma bring the wrath of Marco on this whole fucking city. I'm talkin some new age apocalypse type shit. That's my word."

Fatts was enjoying his friend's tirade. "I already know. That's why I fucks wit you."

Chapter 9

It had been a little over a week since the Olive Garden shooting. The doctors were successfully able to stop Ebony's bleeding just in time to save her life. Unfortunately her trauma sent her into a coma with no timetable on if or when she would recover. For days Gutta stood at her bedside in case she were to wake up. It hurt his heart to see her in a weakened state. She had been his lover and friend since his dingy-clothes petty-larceny days. It also didn't help that he felt responsible for her pain. Even though he didn't know exactly who it was shooting, he was certain the bullet that lodged in Ebony's throat was meant for him. Knowing that, he felt the least could do was stay by her side.

He sat watching *Family Feud* on the hospital TV when he decided to call Gotti. *Ring… Ring…*

"What's good, bruh?"

"What's up? How you know it was me?"

"What? You called from yo phone, right?"

"Oh shit, I'm burnt the fuck out." The brothers enjoyed a good laugh. "How it's going out there, though?"

"Everything forreal, bout to make rounds downtown."

"That's what it is. I just was checking on you. Be safe out there, bruh."

"I already know. How shorty doing, though?"

"She ain't woke up yet, but I'mma hold her down till she do."

"Like a real nigga posed to." With that Gotti ended the call.

Since Gutta was preoccupied with Ebony, he was left to conduct their business alone. Not to mention Money had been missing for the last three days, which was nothing new. He was known for that every now and then. This just meant Gotti had to boss up, which he had no problem with. He rode downtown, heading to pick up his cash from his 36th Street posse.

The entire team had come a long way in the last couple years. The brothers took the blueprint learned from Money and applied it to their neighborhood of Marshall Courts. Lil Man, Tye, and M.A. completely deadbolted the hood. Not a dollar was made unless it was by them or one of their workers. The operation ran nearly identical to Money's River Walk operation. The only flaw was the almost daily shootings that happened around the projects. That was just one aspect of the hood that couldn't be controlled. Fear did nothing to somebody with a gun. The truth was a scared person will shoot faster than a killer would.

Gotti rolled down the 36th Street strip, refreshed by how nice of a day it was. The sun was shining, the wind blowing, and the birds were singing like a Disney movie. Days like this he would've loved to pull out his Bentley. Sadly, he had to get it detailed since Ebony's blood had stained his all-white interior. Lil Boosie's album *Thrilla* bassed from his twelve-inch speakers as he approached the block. *White chalks and blackouts we be dying so young/Murder rate chasing the birth rate in this city I'm from/Fingerprints over the duct tape and his palm on the gun.* Gotti left the system bumping as he hopped out. Lil Man, Tye, and M.A. greeted him with daps and hugs.

"What's up, Gotti? Where Gutta at?" M.A. was smoking a blunt of exotic weed like the laws didn't apply.

"He at Sentara wit Ebony."

"Oh yeah. That's fucked up they did shorty like that."

"I know. Gutta want blood for that shit though."

"Shit, I would too. How a nigga shoot his brother baby mama? That's just stupid."

Gotti paused. He was bewildered by what M.A. could mean. "Who brother? What you know that I don't, fam?"

"Torn shot Ebony. That's Marco brother. I thought you knew that."

"So Marco Ebony baby daddy?"

"Yeah. Where you been, under a rock?"

Gotti was astonished by the information. As long as he knew Ebony, he never thought to ask who her baby daddy was. Until now it was none of his business. Slowly things started to make sense. He knew Marco had a brother named Torn that was doing time somewhere. He just never thought twice about when he got out or what would happen when he did. "So that's who been swinging on us, hunh?"

"Damn, fam, you slipping. Dude been talking bout what he gone do when he catch y'all for the last two weeks. I was bout to slay his ass when I seen him at Hawkins the other day but he had that crazy ass nigga Fatts with him and I only had ten shots."

Gotti was becoming vexed by this new revelation. "Yo, where he be at?"

"I heard he be uptown, but he been robbing niggas all week so he probably laid low."

"You telling me I'm beefin wit a jack boy really?"

"Yeah, he caught a sting for almost a hundred grand yesterday, though I know a lil jaint that got his number too."

"Get it for me right quick."

M.A. pulled his iPhone, dialing his newest fling's number. After a short conversation, he hung up and handed the phone to Gotti. Open to the contacts section, the phone displayed Torn's number. Gotti hit send.

"Yo, who dis?" Torn answered on the second ring.

"You should know. You was looking for me, right?"

"Who the fuck is you?"

"Young Gotti, nigga."

Torn's blood boiled like water in a microwave. "You damn right I'm lookin for you, bitch. You killed my brother."

"Nah, my nigga, yo brother committed suicide wit his smart ass mouth. Look like it run in the family."

"I bet he said more than that bitch saying." Torn was referring to Ebony.

"I'm talking to a dead man right now anyway. I got fifty thousand on this nigga top. Straight up." Gotti was talking to his team, making sure Torn heard the price on his head.

Torn chuckled. "Make sure you keep yo receipt, my nigga. You couldn't see me wit a microscope."

"Oh, I see you, my nigga. I see you so good I'mma paint the city wit you." With that Gotti ended the call, passing the phone back to M.A. "I want y'all to put that tag out there. Somebody gotta die, my nigga. Word." The three captains nodded at their general's request.

Five minutes later Gotti left the hood with the bag of cash he came to collect. He drove the back streets of Wickham Avenue on his way to 21st. Out of nowhere he noticed a gray

Crown Victoria following him. Immediately he gripped the handle of the Glock in his lap.
Through further observation he viewed the two white officers. He stashed his pistol in the hidden
stash box just as they activated their blue-and-red lights. Knowing he didn't have any open
warrants, he pulled over with his license and registration handy.

An eerie feeling came over him as two Jim Carey-looking cops strolled up to his car,
hands already pressed against their weapons. He rolled his window down quickly, handing them
the paperwork. "What you doing wit that? I know exactly who you is, Mr. Jaxavier Walker."

Gotti was frustrated with the cops' recitement of his first and last name. "If you don't
need my license, what you pull me over for? I'm all out of donuts."

The white officers grinned like the Grinch who stole Christmas. "You might not got no
donuts but you definitely sweet enough. Now get yo black ass out the car."

For a second Gotti thought of bucking on the racist pigs but decided against it as pictures
of the Rodney King beating flashed through his brain. Not wanting to get his clothes dirty or deal
with a bunch of trumped-up charges, he exited the car with his arms raised in the hands-up-
don't-shoot pose. The officers aggressively threw him against his truck. With excessive force
they twisted his arms behind his back, slapping the cold cuffs tightly against his wrist. Gotti sat
in the back seat of the Crown Victoria, fuming at the victimization.

Down at the precinct he was escorted to a refrigerated interrogation room. There he spent
the next three hours without the courtesy of even having the cuffs removed from his wrist.
Mentally drained, he laid his head against the cold steel table and dozed off.

Sometime later he was jarred awake by the slamming of the door as the same arresting
officers entered. "Mr. Walker, let me introduce myself. I'm Detective Charles Brodey and this is

my partner, Detective Lance Spider." The one called Detective Spider grabbed Gotti's wrists, removing the cuffs. "I'm sorry about that. Would you like a cigarette or maybe a cup of coffee?"

Gotti wasn't amused by their half-cocked attempts at playing the good guy/bad guy role. "Fuck nah, I don't want no coffee. The first thing I want is a lawyer."

"Hold on, don't put the chicken before the egg. We not even arresting you…yet." Detective Brodey sat in the foldout chair across from Gotti. "Now just answer these few fairly simple questions and we can all be on our way."

Gotti stayed silent. He figured as long as he let them talk, they would be the ones actually answering his unspoken questions. Brodey tossed a manila envelope on the table. "Open it." Gotti didn't budge. Brodey leaned in, spreading a stack of eight-by-ten photos over the table. "Do you know who that is, Gotti? It is Gotti, right?"

"Nah, my name Jaxavier Walker and no, I don't know who that is."

"Hum, that's funny, cause that's totally contrary to the information we received."

"Oh yeah?"

"Yeah, a little birdie told me you were the one who pulled the trigger on Mr. Marcus Knight here. I'm not even gone lie, when I heard it was for a measly two hundred dollars I almost didn't believe him, but when I read your history, wow! I mean countless homicide investigations, drugs, extortion. I just figured crazy muthafuckas like you would kill for anything."

"Look, I told you I don't know him. Now if you happen to run across my lawyer on the way out, you be sure to inform him on what your lil birdie told you."

Detective Spider pulled his chair next to Gotti. "Listen, I could care less about this petty drug dealer." He slid the photos of Marco to the side. "I can't lie, the evidence is not looking good for you. Now all you gotta do is tell us something, anything. You wanna go to jail or you wanna go home?"

Gotti just shook his head. Detective Brodey sat back. "What you gotta say for yourself?"

"All I gotta say is I wanna fuck yo daughter."

"Oh, you a smart ass, hunh? Well, look, I got something smart for you. We got a motive, we got a description, and we got an informant, so go home, make love to whatever slut you lay up with every night, hug whatever horse you rode in on, cause the next time I see you, you'll be an inmate of Newport News city jail. For now you can go, but I won't say goodbye, I'll just say I'll see you later."

Gotti was disgusted. It took everything in him not to crack the racist officer's skull like a sunflower seed. Instead he rose and power-walked as fast as he could out of Satan's lair.

Outside the precinct, the first thing Gotti did was call Mia. "Hey, baabby!" Answering on the first ring, Mia was ecstatic to hear her man's voice.

"What's up, girl. You at the house or nah?"

Mia quickly sensed the panic in Gotti's voice. "I'm home, baby, why? What's wrong?"

"Look, I need you to grab the spare key to the Range and go pick it up for me."

"From where?"

"It's on Thirtieth and Wickham. I need you to do that now, though."

Mia, being the woman she was, had already slipped on some shoes and was halfway out the door. "I'm on it, Gotti, but I need to know what's up asap, aight?"

"Aight, love, I'mma hit you later."

"Kay, bae... Love."

Gotti ended the call, immediately scrolling down to Gucci's number. The phone rang three times before she answered. "Hey, bruh. What's up?"

"I need you to come get me, yo, I got pulled over."

"Where? Where you at? I need to bring bail money or nah?"

"Nah, sis, I'm out. Come get me from over town at the bus station by the shipyard."

"Aight, I'm on my way. Stay there, Gotti, forreal."

"I'mma be there. Yo, hurry up."

Gotti made his way to the bus station, dissecting the words of Detective Brodey. He always had a knack for determining when someone was bluffing. Unfortunately, as he stared into the eyes of the racist detective, he saw the look of a man holding four spades and just waiting for the fifth. For years the 36th Street murder stained his thoughts. Every time he pulled the trigger on one of his enemies, Marco's eyes would always be the ones staring back at him. Until now Gotti had completely suppressed those thoughts. Today, as he sat at the bus station, his anxiety was at an all-time high.

Ten minutes later Gucci arrived, honking the horn on her champagne-colored BMW 745 LI. As soon as he entered the car, she went straight in interrogating him, worse than the previous detectives. "What happened, Gotti? What you do wrong? And how you get out?"

"Yo, yo, chill. Is you gone let me talk or what?"

"Aight, talk."

"I got pulled over downtown but they was talking about some bullshit homicide."

"Homicide! What homicide?"

"Sis, calm down, you blowing me right now. I don't need you yelling in my ear."

Gucci took a deep breath. "Sorry, bruh. I just can't lose my family, Gotti. Not now. I can't take it." Gucci's hand shook on the steering wheel like the car needed a new axle.

"Relax, sis, I ain't going nowhere. That's my word. Just trust me. If they had something, I wouldn't be here talking to you."

"I trust you, yo."

"I know you do. Anyway, where Money at?"

Gucci shrugged her shoulders. "I don't know. He always find the wrong time to do this dumb shit."

"Aight, take me to holla at Gutta."

The siblings were relatively silent on their way to the hospital. Bryson Tiller's album *True to Self* played through the speakers, easing their tensions. Turning into the parking lot of Sentara, the duo noticed a very familiar Phantom parked three spaces from the entrance. Simultaneously they gave each other a confused look. Gucci was furious. Without a word she hopped out the BMW, storming towards Ebony's room. Gotti had to nearly jog to keep pace with her.

Money sat in the waiting room, having an isolated conversation with Gutta when the brother-sister pair emerged from the elevator. Gucci stepped directly in his face with her arms folded across her chest. "Excuse me, but what rock you crawled the fuck from under?"

Money rose from his seat. "I was out of town. Why? When you start questioning me and shit?"

"Since I became fed up wit yo bullshit."

"Whatever, yo."

Money attempted to walk away but Gucci wasn't having it. Every step he took she matched, blocking his escape route. "Nigga, you not brushing me off. You ain't call or nothing. I hope you here to get some penicillin. Wit yo trifling ass."

Money was trying his best to restrain his temper. He stepped closer, pointing his finger in her forehead. "Tierra, I ain't talking bout this shit no more."

Gotti used his arm to back Money up. "Y'all chill. Let's get out this hospital. I need to holla at niggas anyway."

Gucci was choking back tears as she stormed towards the emergency stairwell. Money shook his head. "Shorty crazy forreal."

"That's sis though." Gotti stared straight into Money's eyes. His solemn expression clearly relayed his unspoken threats.

The three generals strolled through the parking lot towards Gucci, who was sitting on her trunk, smoking a cigarette. Gotti wrapped his arm around her shoulder. "You good, sis?"

"Yeah, I'm good, thanks."

"Anyway, look, I got pulled over on the Wick earlier." The group's anticipation rose. "I'm good but they was asking me bout Marco."

Gutta's heart sank to the pit of his stomach. "What about Marco?"

"You already know. They was tossing pictures around, talking bout they got a witness."

"You believe 'em? They could just be fishing."

Money's question created doubt in Gotti's mind. "I don't know, dawg. It been three years and I ain't hear nothing. Why now? Somebody gotta had said something. On top of that, I found out Marco brother Torn the one that hit Ebony."

"Torn the little nigga that caught that body back in the day."

"Yeah, he got out a few weeks ago."

Gutta was livid. "Fuck him. I guess he traded one box for another one."

"You already know."

Money quietly digested all the information, pondering an approach to their current situation. "It's too much going on wit y'all right now. We gotta disappear and give all this heat time to blow over."

Gucci couldn't believe what she was hearing. "Excuse me, disappear? You just got back. That won't enough for you?"

"Chill, shorty. The way you been acting, I wouldn't dare leave you behind for to come back and you done did some left eye shit."

Gucci smiled like it was Christmas morning. Jumping off the trunk, she wrapped her arms around Money's neck. "Aww... Baby, you so sweet."

"I know, especially when you get your way, right?"

"So what's wrong with that?"

"Spoiled ass. Y'all niggas grab somebody too. I ain't gone be the only one bringing sand to the beach."

Gucci stepped back, smacking Money on the arm. "You always fucking up a good moment."

The group burst into laughter. All except Gutta, who had Ebony on his mind. Gotti looked at his brother. Their sibling telepathy told him exactly what was on his mind. "Yo, I'mma come dolo. Me and Gutta just gone chill while y'all booed up."

"Hell nah, my nigga, you gotta bring Mia. She ain't going for that shit."

"She be aight. I'd rather chill wit you anyway."

"Come on, bruh. I'm good. Bring Mia." Gutta's tone insisted that Gotti comply.

"Aight, fam. Money, where we going anyway?"

"Let me handle that. Just bring yo passports." With that the guys dapped and departed, going their separate ways.

Gutta went back to the hospital to pay Ebony one more visit before they left. Standing beside her bed, he secretly prayed that her eyes would just pop open. His arm hair stood on end, listening to the beeping of her heart monitor. Sadly, that was the only evidence that his love was still among the living. "Damn, shorty, it's true when they say you never know what you got till it's gone. Remember how you always used to hit me wit them old ass quotes? I feel that shit now. I need you to wake up, Ebony, for real. I need my Beyoncé back. God willing, though, right? But check this, I gotta leave for a minute, but soon as I come back, you gone be the first face I kiss. I love you, yo. Stay sweet, stay smart, and stay safe, aight?" He bent down, placing a passionate kiss on her forehead. His eyes glistened as he exited the room, prepared for whatever the world had in store.

* * *

Gotti arrived at his 6,000-square-foot Yorktown estate in Gucci's BMW. The five-bedroom, four-and-a-half bath luxury home was equipped with a movie theater, home studio, game room, and a backyard infinity pool. The marble floors, high ceilings, and extravagant

furniture transformed the spot into a place that any of society's elite would be proud to call

home. Gotti pushed the button for his privacy fence to roll back. In the driveway was his

platinum Range, parked behind Mia's rare 2012 Lexus LFA supercar.

Pulling up behind the Range, he hopped out, rushing to the truck. The only thing that was

on his mind was the cash he had just collected from his 36th Street posse. Opening the back

passenger door, Gotti looked on the floor where the bag was supposed to be, finding nothing but

an old McDonald's cup. His blood pressure began to elevate. Before he panicked, he went

through the entire car, removing everything but the seats and steering wheel. Still the bag was

nowhere in sight.

In his last grasp at hope, he twisted the knob on his designed stone front door. Ascending

the floating staircase, he headed straight to the master bedroom, where Mia spent majority of her

time. She was startled when he barged in with a deranged look on his face. "Yo, you ain't see no

bag in the truck?"

"Wha... What bag?"

"Any bag, Mia, did you see any bag in the back seat of the car?"

"No, I didn't see nothing back there."

"Did you look?"

"Why would I, Gotti? You didn't tell me to look."

The fearful look on Mia's face softened Gotti's anger. He knew she would never take

anything from him and didn't want her to think he didn't trust her in any way. "Damn, bae, I'm

sorry. I'm buggin right now. I ain't trynna come at you crazy tho."

"I know, love, everything just hectic for you, right? Sit down and talk to me."

Gotti took a seat on the edge of the bed. Mia came up behind him, massaging his shoulders tenderly. Her touch quickly eased his tensions. "Shit going left, Mia, no bullshit. I don't know what the fuck going on."

"What happened, Gotti? Stop spinning me in circles."

"First I got stopped by some whack ass police. I'm thinking they on some bullshit and they come at me talking bout a old ass body."

"A body! Oh my God, bae! What you do?" Mia went from calm to hysterical in two seconds flat.

"Yo, cool it, shorty, everything good. They was just questioning a nigga."

"So you not going to jail?"

"No, Mia, I'm not going to jail."

"Oh, so what was in the bag?"

"Just some money but it ain't nothing that can't be replaced."

"The way you was acting, I might need to put in for public housing."

Mia's comment caused Gotti to burst into laughter. "Yo, you fuckin silly. That shit ain't bout nothing, though. Some fuckin winos probly broke in my shit."

"Probly. You know how cruddy downtown is."

"Yeah. Look, pack some clothes right quick."

"Pack for what? Where we going?"

"On a vacation."

Chapter 10

Torn, Fatts, Bud, and Row pulled up to the Seven Oaks apartment complex in Torn's brand new forest-green Land Rover Defender. They had just come from Farmville, Virginia, where CO Lakeisha Hubbard was having her 23rd birthday party. Originally Torn was skeptical about going to the rural town, but was persuaded by the promise that it would be a small gathering with only a few of her closest friends. Torn agreed to attend, recruiting a few of his most loyal soldiers to accompany him.

Unbeknownst to them, the party was a complete freak fest. Lakeisha and her three female clique had cameras stationed on tripods throughout the entire house. X-rated pornographic videos played on various televisions throughout the dwelling. The party evolved into one big orgy with Torn and his posse taking advantage of the promiscuous females in more positions than an advanced version of *Kama Sutra* could outline. For 48 hours straight the females were passed around like tortilla bowls at a Super Bowl party.

They were on their way back to the city when Torn's Uncle Foots called, informing him he had a house full of smokers ready to spend their entire checks on crack. Not willing to let any money elude him, Torn quickly accepted. Uncle Foots was a slinky six-foot-six dude resembling the retired basketball player Kareem Abdul Jabbar. His house was the local trap house where many drug addicts came for their daily fix. Marco, before he died, was the main supplier for the apartment. Coincidentally, Seven Oaks was located directly across from Marshall Courts, so close that since Gotti and Gutta controlled that hood, they also controlled Seven Oaks. Fully aware of this, Torn and his gang stayed completely alert, even though the back-to-back blunts they smoked had them high as Goodyear blimps.

Foots greeted the posse as soon as they approached the door, smiling like they were delivering Publishers Clearinghouse checks. "What's up, nephew!"

"Ain't shit. What's good wit you, unc?"

"You know me, trynna get a deal like a broke bitch in a corner store. What you gone do for me?"

"Goddamn. We ain't even made no bread yet."

"Come on. You know I need a pick-me-up, nephew."

"Aight, man, we ain't doing this all night, though. You gotta come up wit some bread too."

Torn gave Bud the nod to give Foots a bump. Bud went into the living room where six customers waited, jittery to be served. The remaining three hustlers sat around the kitchen table, drinking Heinekens and smoking weed. Torn was faded to the max as he observed his homie exchanging the bags of crack for various dingy-looking bills. "Ay, Foots, come here right quick."

"What's good, nephew? You cappin my flow right now."

"I ain't trynna hear that shit. Come here." Foots hurried to see what Torn wanted. "Answer this for me. Why would you call me all the way out here when Gotti and Gutta got work all up and down this strip?"

"Nephew, I owe them niggas everything down to Grandma Pomeranian. That bridge cut and burned already."

"Word, I feel you."

Suddenly Bud came rushing into the kitchen. He was obviously blown away by something. "What's up, yo." Torn sat up, prepared to spring into action.

"Nah, nah, ain't nothing like that. You see that skinny brown-skinned lady wit the good hair?"

Torn looked past Bud into the living room. Immediately he spotted her sucking on the glass stem like it was a clogged-up Slurpee straw. "Yeah, what about her?"

"Sooo I'm in there counting the bread, making sure everything straight, right?"

"Right."

"Okay, she gets to running off at the mouth, all reckless and shit, bragging bout her sons and how they run this shit, the whole neighborhood theirs, she the queen, all that dumb shit. So I ask the bitch who her sons is. Guess what she say?"

A devilish smiled spread over Torn's face. "Gotti and Gutta."

"Bingo." Torn's mouth salivated as he looked back to Ms. Tina like she was a bowl of Lucky Charms at the end of a rainbow. "What, you trynna snatch her up or what?" Bud was ready to bag and tag his newly discovered prey.

"Nah, my nigga, that's too simple. We ain't taking that dusty ass bitch nowhere." Torn took one last puff of his blunt before heading to the living room. Ms. Tina was completely spaced out. Slowly opening her eyes, she saw Torn and Bud towering over her. "What's up, shorty? What you say yo name was?"

"I'm Ms. Tina, baby, how you doin?"

"Ms. Tina, they call me Torn. I was trynna see if you could help me out wit something."

"What is it?"

"See, my homeboy here just came home from a long jail bit. You know, he a lil rusty. I'm trynna see if you can give him a lil taste right quick."

"Oh nah, baby, I just don't be trickin wit no anybody, I'm sorry."

Torn reached in his pocket, pulling out a clear bag containing an ounce of the addictive drug. Holding it in the air, he displayed it for the addict. "You sure?"

Ms. Tina stared at the bag like it was the original Holy Grail. She contemplated her decision. She had tricked before but never with somebody she didn't know and definitely never with somebody her sons' age. If they ever found out, hell would have a white Christmas. "Baby, my sons would turn us into cold cases if they knew I was even thinking about disgracing them like that."

"They ain't gotta know, mama. We pretty good at keeping secrets."

Ms. Tina looked at the bag one more time. The temptation spoke volumes, overriding her conscience. "Look, I'mma do it this one time, but I'm telling you, if my sons find out, you might as well dig yo graves, and dig me one while y'all at it."

Torn held up two fingers. "Scout's honor."

"Aight, come on."

Torn handed Ms. Tina the entire bag of crack. "Go head, mama, he gone meet you up there." The two tempters watched as Ms. Tina nearly skipped up the stairs, anxious to board the Starship Enterprise.

"Yo, you know I ain't fuckin shorty, right?"

Torn gave Bud a criticizing look. "Come on, my nigga, tighten up. You know damn well I wouldn't tell you do no shit like that."

Twenty minutes later Bud and Row entered the upstairs bedroom where Ms. Tina was sprawled across the bed, faded from nearly overdosing on the powerful drugs. "This bitch sleep."

"Hell nah, she just high as shit."

Equipped with rope and duct tape, they quickly tied her arms and legs to the four bedposts. "Where this nigga at?" Bud questioned to no one in particular.

Row, who was leaning against the dresser smoking a cigarette, shrugged his shoulders. "I don't know. Torn burnt the fuck out. He probably forgot we was up this bitch."

"We should've just killed her."

"If he ain't here in the next two minutes, I'mma just kill her anyway."

"Word, I'm wit you on that one."

Hearing the voices around her, Ms. Tina groggily opened her eyes. Pulling on her restraints, she noticed her limbs would not move. "Hold up. What's all this?"

"Just relax, you gone be aight."

"Nah, this won't part of the deal. Let me go."

"Now why would I tie you up just to let you go?"

"Let me go! Foots! Foots!"

Bud nodded his head to Row. Unraveling the duct tape, Row pressed a long strip tightly across her mouth. The experience completely sobered Ms. Tina. Tears began streaking down her cheeks.

Three minutes later the doorknob turned. Torn and Fatts entered, carrying a large pot with them. Fatts had on oven mitts as he placed the pot on the dresser. "Don't tell me y'all niggas cooking while we up here babysitting," Bud said, perplexed by the container.

"Come on, man. Every time I think you can't say anything dumber, you totally redeem yourself." Torn laughed heavily at his own joke.

"That shit ain't that funny."

"I'm fucking wit you, my nigga. Get out yo feelings."

Row lifted the top off the pot. Inside was cooking oil so hot the steam nearly scorched his eyebrows. "Damn, what, you bout to burn her? That's fucked up, Torn."

"Oh yeah? If you think that's fucked up, I can only imagine what you feel about this." Torn reached in his pocket, displaying a plastic funnel.

Row's mouth dropped. "Nah."

Torn smiled. "Yeah." Walking over to a sobbing Ms. Tina, Torn kneeled beside her head. "Just relax, mama. It's gone all be over soon. You know, I always heard that the children will pay for the sins of their parents. Nobody ever talks about what happens when the roles are reversed. It probably ain't no way to prepare for this shit anyway. Damn." He kissed Ms. Tina on her forehead before he rose. "Aight, y'all ready? One of y'all gotta lift her back off the bed, and one of y'all gotta hold this funnel. I got the pot. Fatts, you record on yo phone."

"I'mma hold her back cause y'all niggas crazy." Row volunteered for the lesser of two evils. Bud grabbed the funnel and shoved it in Ms. Tina's vagina.

Torn put the oven mitts on. With both hands he held the pot, ready to siphon the blistering grease. "Yo, stick that shit deeper, she ain't no virgin." Bud rammed the entire tube of the funnel into Ms. Tina's opening. Torn took one deep breath before tilting the pot, mercilessly draining the hot grease into the tube.

The scene was repulsive. Ms. Tina violently bucked as the acid filled her insides. The torrid liquid incinerated her organs. Her pain was unbearable. Her curdling screams were muffled by the thick duct tape, and her efforts to free herself proved frivolous. Inwardly she prayed for death, hoping to end her torment. After close to a minute, the trauma became too much for her body, causing her to fade out of consciousness.

When finished, the torturers descended the stairs to find a panicking Foots. "Damn, unc, what's wrong wit you?"

"What you do to that lady, nephew? She ain't done nothing wrong."

"Don't sweat it, she good."

Foots had tears in his eyes. "Nephew, you know who mama that is? You just put a bullet in both our heads. What's wrong wit you?"

"Who you talking bout? Gotti? Why you ain't tell them niggas that when they shot my brother? Matter of fact, don't answer that." Torn pulled his gun and pointed it at Foots' head. In one motion he pulled the trigger, twisting his uncle's cap like a 20-ounce Sprite bottle. Foots was dead before he hit the floor.

The night was calm as Row led the pack from the apartment, followed by Fatts, Torn, and Bud bringing up the rear. Suddenly an mysterious sensation flowed through Fatts' body, causing him to stop before he reached the bottom of the porch steps. His hand instinctively eased towards his gun. *Boom!* Row, unfortunately leading the way, was the first to get hit, dropping like a puppet with the strings cut. Panic passed through the gang as a variety of shots followed, sending the remaining three crawling on the pavement in desperate need of shelter. Luckily they found it beside the closest vehicle they saw.

Tye, along with three of his soldiers, had set an unexpected ambush. For hours they patiently waited for their marks to exit. Tye, being the leader of the group, was the first to fire, grabbing the life from Row in an instant. That shot was the cue for Smoke and Steve to follow, sending a flurry of bullets in the direction of their enemies.

"Fuck! Nigga, they hit Row." Torn was distraught over the loss of his most trusted soldier.

"Fuck that, we gotta make it to the Rover." Bud clinched his .44 Bulldog, ready to make his gun bark.

Fatts was crouched on the other side of Bud. He was paying vital attention to the bullets' trajectory, attempting to pinpoint which direction the shots were coming from. After mapping the shooters' location, he concocted a plan of attack. "Bud, look, I'mma cover fire for you, but you gotta run back through the house and come out the other side. One of them niggas on that corner right there. You should be able to get behind him. Then you already know what to do."

"Don't seem like I got a choice. Let's get it." Bud got himself ready to sprint back to the house. Fatts and Torn made sure he was set before they popped up, firing rapidly in random directions, drawing the opposition's attention. Bud then took off, leaping over Row's corpse and diving through the apartment's door. Feeling pressured by their enemies' attack, the hit squad returned a hail of bullets.

Bud scrambled his way through the house, emerging out the front door. In the distance he noticed a human figure on one knee, peeping in the opposite direction. Keeping low, he stealthily made his way to the end of the building. Steve, kneeled in his marksman position, was oblivious to the impending danger. Bud attempted to get close as possible to his target. Suddenly Steve looked back. In one swift motion he charged Bud, mushing him in the face while grabbing ahold of the vicious revolver. Bud's heart pounded, hoping his sneak attack wouldn't be the cause of his untimely demise. With his one free hand, he pushed Steve back as hard as he possibly could. The force repelled Steve in the opposite direction. His grasp on the revolver loosened. Bud, seeing his window of opportunity, wasted no time before he squeezed a shot that dropped Steve like a wrecked automobile in a junkyard.

Smoke watched the whole episode in slow motion from his position across the parking lot. The death of his right hand sent him into a murderous rage. The reverberation of his Taurus numbed his palm as he relentlessly finger-popped the trigger. Ducking behind the building, Bud patiently waited for his chance to reappear. *Click.* The gunfire from Smoke silenced. His Taurus clip was hollow. The realization pleased Bud. Veering around the building, he had his target solely in his crosshairs. With one flick of his finger, he released a powerful bullet into Smoke's chest that pushed him back like the impact from a sumo wrestler.

The termination of his collaborators left Tye the last man standing to attempt the seemingly impossible. The city quieted. In the distance a slew of police sirens could be heard. Unfortunately his thirst for blood was unquenched. Breathing deep breaths, he was prepared to abandon his position and continue his assault. With his hand on the trigger of his .40 caliber Desert Eagle, he heard car doors slam. His targets had all hopped in Torn's Land Rover and were making their escape. Conveniently, to leave the parking lot, Torn had to ride directly past him. Knowing this, he waited. As the fleeing truck passed, he readily riddled the vehicle with massive-sized bullet holes that nearly catapulted the transportation. The occupants all ducked as the car swerved down the street, barely escaping Ty's wrath.

* * *

"Welcome to Jamaica." Gotti, Mia, Gucci, Money, Gutta, and Carla departed Kingston International Airport. Immediately they were greeted by a thin Jamaican holding a sign that read 'Walker.' The travel agent who planned their trip hired the limousine driver to escort the travelers to the Marriott Resort. There each couple had a villa reserved in their name.

Gutta invited one of his side pieces along. He knew everybody would feel awkward if he didn't. Carla was a light-brown-skinned, five-six, 130-pound exotic dancer who favored the singer Rihanna with a slightly curvier figure. Like most females from her demographic, she had never been on a vacation out of the States. The rows of coconut trees along the path that led to the hotel mesmerized her. "Damn, Gutta, this shit the bomb, ain't it, beau." Her gaze was fixed out the limousine's window.

"Yeah," Gutta responded nonchalantly. He and Carla had been having casual sex for about a year. Her willingness to completely submit to his will earned her the title of his main mistress. The fact that she was easy on the eyes and had an amazing twat earned her extra points with him. That being said, she still didn't hold a candle to Ebony. Ebony was from the streets and conducted herself like a lady at all times. Carla, on the other hand, was also from the streets but conducted herself like you would expect a hood rat to.

Gucci rested her head on Money's shoulder, exhausted from the long flight. She could tell by Gutta's demeanor that Carla was really irritating him. "So, Carla, how long you knew my brother?" she asked, bringing the girl's attention back to the car.

"Bout two years but we been together for almost a year now." Gutta shook his head at her overexaggeration of their relationship.

"That's funny, cause I see Gutta all the time and I ain't never seen you." Gucci was intentionally demeaning the ghetto escort.

"You know how he is, all secretive and shit."

"Yeah, I know. Where you work at, though?"

"Shiiit, girl, I work at Liquid Blue. You know, the one on Dresden."

"Do you know of another one?"

"I guess not, hunh." The dim-witted Carla laughed at her own expense. Gucci's displeasure was evident as she attempted to force a smile.

The couples arrived at their hotel about an hour later. They all made their way to the villas, agreeing to meet later. Gucci had insisted they do some activities together before the day was out.

Carla was happier than a toddler in Willy Wonka's chocolate factory as she entered the villa. After kicking her shoes off, she jumped straight on the bed like she was still five years old. In all her life she had never been privileged to so much luxury. The villa was laced with imported Egyptian carpet, plush furniture, and paintings of African queens on every wall. The bed she bounced on was a king-sized pillow-top Tempur-Pedic with a solid gold canopy and lace coverings. The spacious kitchen area and large bathroom outfitted with a full-sized jacuzzi was just as exquisite as the rest of the villa. Money had spared no expense on the vacation dwellings.

Gutta sat on the plush recliner, twisting a blunt of some exotic Jamaican ganja. During the ride the limousine driver had sold him an ounce from his personal stash. He ignored Carla as she made her way from room to room, taking selfies wherever she stopped. "Bae, this shit better than my mama whole house." She swan-dived on the comfortable bed.

"Yo, come here right quick," Gutta said, putting fire to his finger-sized blunt, filling his lungs with the potent drug. She quickly obliged. Softly sitting on Gutta's lap, she grabbed the blunt from his mouth, inhaling a mouthful of smoke herself. Carla grinded her cushioned bottom against his lap, causing his manhood to press against his jeans, begging for a release. "What's up, shorty? You brush this horse, you betta be ready to mount this muthafucka." Gutta grabbed the blunt out of Carla's mouth, placing it between his lips.

"What you talking bout, daddy? I ain't even did nothing." She began seductively kissing on his neck.

Gutta caressed Carla's velvety thigh, guiding his hand up her sheer dress. Moving her lace panties to the side, he slid two fingers into her already dripping pussy. Carla released a deep seductive gasp. Repeating his in-and-out motion, he rapidly finger-popped her, only slowing up to massage her clit. She was in pure ecstasy. With her eyes closed, she caressed and squeezed her firm breast. This foreplay continued for the next couple minutes until Gutta couldn't take it anymore. Pushing Carla off his lap, he stood up, undoing his YSL belt buckle and dropping his Balmain jeans to the floor. Spinning his muse by her arm, he bent her over the back of the now unreclined recliner. Fully inflamed, she placed both her knees in the seat, arching her back to allow Gutta full access.

With his blunt still between his lips, he spread Carla's butt cheeks, penetrating her warm slit with his rock-hard genitalia. "Ah!... Ah!... Ah!" Carla's moans were in sync with Gutta's thrust as he viciously pounded her from the back. The loud clapping of their bodies banging had both participants on the brink of eruption. Gutta increased his speed, hammering Carla's vagina like an overzealous construction worker. "Ahh!... Ahh... Ahh! Ooo!... Fuck!" Carla thrust her rump backwards, colliding with Gutta's thighs, sending him over the edge. Feeling the tingling sensation in his penis, he pulled out, dumping a bucket of warm semen on her buttocks with some shooting to her back.

His breathing was heavy as he pulled his pants up and checked his watch. "Come on, let's hit this shower. We gotta meet the others in forty-five minutes." Carla, still in pain from the savage lovemaking session, gingerly made her way to the bathroom.

The group met up an hour later at the Jamaican Soul Food Café located in the lobby of the resort. The men were in full vacation gear. Money wore a Lacoste button-up shirt, Lacoste khaki shorts, Lacoste low-cut sneakers, and a Miami Marlins baseball cap. Gutta and Gotti both dressed similarly with Polo v-neck t-shirts and Polo khaki shorts. The only difference was Gotti wore a Polo bucket hat with all-white Air Force Ones and Gutta a Gucci bucket with Gucci shoes and the belt to match. The females all wore two-piece bathing suits. Gucci covered her bathing suit with a sheer t-shirt and a miniskirt. Mia wore a fishnet dress over hers, while Carla, who just didn't see the need to cover hers at all, was convinced to at least wear a scarf around her waist.

The native waitress approached the table to take their order. She was a beautiful Rastafarian lady with her long dreads tucked in a duby wrap like Erykah Badu. "Hey mon! Welcome to de Soul Food Café. Ya ready to order or ya wan me come back?"

Gucci, claiming she was starving, was the first to respond, ordering the curry chicken special with dirty rice and a large sweet tea. Money, who was seated next, ordered the jerked chicken with a side of cocoa bread. Gotti and Gutta both ordered beef patties with fries and carrot juice, which they picked up from visits at their ethnic grandparents' house. Carla, who was baffled by majority of the items on the menu, settled for a cheeseburger and fries with a large Sprite.

"What the agent line up for us today?" Mia directed her question to Money.

"First I reserved y'all a slot at this island spa out by the beach."

Gucci near snapped her neck to look at Money. "What you mean y'all?"

"Don't start this shit, Gucci. We gotta go handle some business, then we gone link up wit y'all at the beach before we hit the reggae club."

"I knew yo ass was up to something, trynna ditch us like we some silly bitches, but it's all good." Gucci sat back, pouting, with her arms folded across her chest.

"Shit, girl, I need a spa treatment. Massages, facials, and they free. I don't know why you tripping, we winning." Carla held her hand up for a high five.

Gucci just stared at her like she still had used toilet paper on her palm. "See what I'm talking bout?"

"Chill out, sis, we ain't gone leave y'all for long," Gotti said, attempting to ease Gucci's anger.

"I ain't feeling that shit neither, girl, but don't even trip. We gone be good. Let 'em not come back." Mia held Gotti's American Express credit card in the air, waving it back and forth. Gotti brushed Mia's threats off.

The couples ate and chatted for the next hour before departing. The girls headed to the beach and the guys got into a waiting black Denali positioned in front of the hotel. The black Denali transported them to the Grassroots. The local strip club was popular for having the sexiest dancers on the island. Money learned of its existence through one of his associates. Since his very first visit, he vowed to attend whenever he was able. The building resembled a vintage church. The enormous stone front steps led to two large wooden doors that served as the club's entrance.

Swinging the doors open, the brothers were astonished. A smorgasbord of beautiful Jamaican women trotted through the dwelling as bare as the day they were born. After paying the entry fee, they were seated at a round table. Immediately a brown-sugar-colored native with shoulder-length golden dreads and coconuts covering her nipples and vagina approached. "How ya doin, star, ya wan sumting to drink?" Money ordered three shots of Patrón, pre-tipping the waitress with a one-hundred-dollar bill. Joyfully she walked away with her buttocks jiggling like Bill Cosby's Jell-O. "Shorty the shit, ain't she, fam." Gotti was stuck in a trance as his eyes followed her exit. "Yeah, my nigga, these clubs ain't nothing like the ones back home. Every shorty that work here stacked. That shit like a requirement," Money informed.

"I see why you wanted to slide off."

"Just cause we bring sand to the beach don't mean we gotta build a castle wit it." The trio laughed.

"I'm definitely wit you on that."

As if on cue, three of the sexiest Jamaican dancers in the club approached, wearing G-strings and nothing else. "Ya wan dance?"

Gutta readily pulled out his cash, flashing his numerous denominations. "Show me how them bands make y'all dance." The other two followed suit, pulling out their cash as the ladies dropped their G-strings and put on a show to Sean Paul's "Gimme the Light."

Behind the wall a well-known Rasta by the name of Damian Danger was focused on their every moves. From the moment they stepped in the club, he had his video security system following them. "Wha da American rude boy doing on me island, star?" He and his two oversized bodyguards scrutinized the visitors. Fifteen minutes of idle watching bored Damian, enticing him to find his answer in a more direct approach.

Money was enjoying his tantalizing lap dance when he felt somebody staring at him. Surveilling the room, his eyes stopped on three Jamaicans observing him from the bar. "Yo, y'all chill right quick, I be right back," he informed the brothers before removing the stripper from his lap and strolling over to the Jamaicans.

"Money, I must've missed ya call, breadren. Wha ya doin in me town?"

Money shook the head Rasta's hand. "Nah, Damian, this ain't a business trip. Me and my brothers out here wit our ladies on vacation."

Damian looked past Money at his compadres. "Still, ya should've called, star. I could've shown ya a better time."

"I appreciate it but it's only a short stay. I just had to show them how shit pop in Jamaica."

"Nonsense, mon. You must stop by de shack for drinks. We talk. Bring ya breadren."

Money knew his back was against the wall. Damian's request was only a formality. Really he was demanding that Money comply. Damian Danger was a legend in the Jamaican culture. Born and raised in the slums of Trenton, he rose to power through the illegal deportation of cocaine and political rifts throughout the island's history. Money was introduced to him when he was only a teen through a guy he considered his mentor. Unfortunately he had burned one too many bridges, leaving Money to fill his shoes as one of Damian's main customers in the States. Through hard work and perseverance, Money eventually elevated to new heights, bypassing his deceased mentor. A lot of it was credited to the commandeering of River Walk.

Although Money and Damian had been doing business for years, his unannounced presence was like a Jay-Z new watch alert to the cautious Jamaican. Business was usually conducted over a payphone, and not once had Money brought anyone to the island with him. Damian was anxious to get to the bottom of this visit. The first step to him was to uncover the identities of the other tourists. The plan was set for Money and his brothers to meet Damian at his estate near Capetown before they returned to the resort.

Less than an hour later the Denali arrived at a wrought-iron gate that encircled a massive estate. The gate was patrolled by two Jamaicans carrying AK-47s on their shoulders while two human-sized Rottweilers roamed freely throughout the grounds. The car waited at the gate until two different Rastas came from the perimeter of the mansion with leashes for the vicious animals. Immediately after, the gate rolled back, allowing the visitors entry to the magnificent estate.

The brothers were truly impressed with the property, which had an intricately manicured lawn with a granite driveway. Pulling to the front of the grand castle, the truck was approached by a dark-skinned, five-nine, 120-pound Jamaican woman with shoulder-length dreads. She was escorted by two brolic male security guards. Tapping her finger on the tinted window, she instructed they roll it down. "Ya wan see Damian, leave ya weapons in de car."

Money looked to the brothers. They both looked back at him and shrugged their shoulders, knowing neither one was armed. The lady watched their every move. One by one the trio stepped out the vehicle and was instantly frisked by one of the muscular Jamaican goons. After being cleared, they were escorted up the marble porch steps to the entrance of the mansion. The brothers were still in awe as they entered the vestibule. In front of them a massive painting of Haile Selassie hung on the wall in a 24-carat-gold frame. They then traveled through the house to the backyard, where a shirtless Damian was. In the light of day, they really noticed how nappy his dreads and facial hair was.

"Money, mon, welcome to me shack." Damian had his arms extended to his associate.

Money embraced the Rasta with a masculine hug. "What's good, fam. Damian, these my bros Gotti and Gutta. Bros, this Damian Danger."

Damian extended his arms to the brothers. "Any breadren of Money I embrace as mi own."

The brothers met his embrace. "Good to meet you too."

"Come, come have a seat, star." Damian directed them to the gold-trimmed patio table with matching gold-trimmed patio chairs. They all sat as a scantily clad Jamaican maid emerged from the mansion. She carried a platter containing three drinks with lemons hanging on the edges. She placed one in front of each individual with a wooden cigar box being placed in the middle. "Drink, star." The brothers waited for Money to sip from his glass before swallowing the alcoholic beverage. The drink went down smooth as distilled water, although it was full of the best rum brewed in Jamaica.

"How it taste, mon? Dat dere de island special iced tea." Damian then slid the box from the middle of the table. Opening the top, he passed branch-sized backwoods around the table. Each one was filled with three grams of exotic ganja. Gutta, anxious to take his edge off, lit the blunt, puffing deeply. The heavy smoke filled his lungs, causing him to double over, attempting

to catch his breath. His coughs were uncontrollable. Damian chuckled. "Wholl on, star, dat dere

da best ganja on de island."

"Goddamn, that shit wild." Gutta was wiping tears from his eyes.

"Money, nuff respect to ya breadren. He a true soldier, mon."

"Yeah, eventually I had planned to introduce them to you. Better sooner than later, I

guess."

"Erryting arry?"

"Always. Like me, they true bosses. In time I plan on them coppin from you personally."

Gotti was stunned at the revelation. They had just met a major overseas connect. The

wheels started turning in his brain. He wondered if Money had truly desired to make them his

equals.

"No ting, star, I and I is one." Damian raised his glass in the air. "Welcome to I family,

breadren." The new inductees raised their glasses before downing the rest of the liquid.

Out of nowhere the duby-wrapped lady from earlier emerged, taking a seat on Damian's

lap. "Money, I don't tink I had de pleasure of introducing you to my heart and soul, Chanta."

"What's up, Chanta," Money greeted the kingpin's wife. Chanta simply nodded.

In her hand was a manila folder she handed to Damian. He inspected the file's contents in

silence before tossing the folder across the table to Gotti. His actions unnerved the skeptic

hustler. One would believe Medusa's head was on the file the way he froze, baffled as to why he

was being presented the file. "Go on." Damian nodded to the folder.

"What's this?" Gotti asked. Reluctantly he took the file in his possession. Inside was a xeroxed newspaper clipping on the murder of Marcus Knight, along with a police report showing the request for a warrant due to the testimony of a confidential informant. After scanning the papers, Gotti tossed the file back on the table. Intently he sat back, waiting to see where this probe was leading.

"Worry not, star. I haffi be aware of erry lion in me kingdom." Gotti remained silent. "I undastand erry rude boy watched by Babylon." Gotti nodded his head, making sure no displeasure displayed in his expression.

The group chatted while finishing their backwoods before getting up to exit. Damian walked his guests to the front porch, escorted by three of his armed security guards. He hugged each one individually before sending them on their way. When he got to Gotti, he held him up. "Gotti, breadren, when I look upon ya, I see the heart of a lion and de eyes of a warrior. Nuff respect to ya, boi. My intelligence no discover the bloodclot serpent who a try to poison ya, mon. Remember, ya watch the water for da sharks a-swarmin, star."

Gotti carefully heeded Damian's words. "Preciate that, Damian."

"No worries, star, erryting arry."

Gotti entered the Denali, reflecting on the day's events. With Damian on his side, he could put his team in position to control the entire city. The opportunity excited him. If he played his cards right, he would be done spending his nights in the jects. From now on he would fly high and spend most of his nights in a jet.

* * *

Back at the resort the girls had been to the spa and received facials and massages. After purchasing lounge chairs from the hotel's lobby shop, they made their way to the beach to enjoy the beautiful weather. "Girl, you wouldn't believe how this thot ass bitch playing herself." Mia was lounging on her phone, engaged in a Facebook beef with one of Gotti's groupies.

"I don't even know why you entertaining that shit anyway." Gucci was on her phone, shopping for shoes.

After being on the beach for 30 minutes, Mia had pulled out Gotti's credit card. After racking up $2,000 worth of clothing, she passed it to Gucci. "Nah, she started the shit. I'm just not gone let no bitch come for me, period."

"Whatever. Tell her how that nigga got you out here frying like steaks at a barbecue."

"If I had something else to do, I wouldn't be on my phone. Y'all boring ass bitches ain't trynna get in the water or nothing."

"Ain't nobody swimming out there wit jellyfish, stingrays, and only God knows what else."

"Gucci, stop it. That water blue as Jay-Z baby name. Ain't nothing in there you ain't gone see coming."

Gucci thought about it for a second before submitting her $700 Prada order. "Aight, come on, but if I get bit by a jellyfish, I'mma beat yo ass."

"I guess it's a good thing jellyfish don't bite, hunh."

The pair pulled their dresses off and ran to the ocean, leaving Carla to babysit their property. Mia was the first one to the water, diving as soon as she got deep enough to swim.

Gucci wasn't far behind, jumping on Mia's back as she tried to come up. Both friends popped right back up, laughing hysterically at Mia's shocking yelp.

As the girls played, Carla was having the time of her life shopping online with Gotti's credit card. She had just finished purchasing a Fendi bag when a tall figure approached, standing in front of her. "Excuse me, you blocking my light." Carla pulled her shades from her eyes. In front of her stood a six-foot-six, muscular-built Jamaican resembling Taye Diggs from *How Stella Got Her Groove Back.*

"Seems to me ya need no light, gorgeous, the flower has already blossomed."

Carla was flattered. "Sorry, you cute and all, but I'm here wit somebody."

The Jamaican scanned the beach with his hands over his eyes like a lifeguard. "I no see no man on the horizon, so tell me what ya called, gal?"

"I'm Carla."

"I'm Dink. Nice ta meet your acquaintance, Carla." Dink grabbed her fingertips, pressing his lips to the back of her hand. Her lower region moistened at the softness of his touch.

"Ahum, scuse me."

Carla looked past Dink to see Gucci and Mia standing there, drying water from their hair with beach towels. The fear on Carla's face exposed her feelings about her suspicious predicament. "Um... Mr. Dink, these my sisters-in-law, Gucci and Mia. Girls, this Dink. He thought I was somebody he knew."

Gucci didn't buy that excuse for a second. "First off, he don't need to know my name, and if I was you, he wouldn't know yours neither." Gucci looked at Carla like she was a scolding parent.

"I mean no harm, beautiful. I just be on my way, no worries." Dink raised his hands in surrender as he backed away from the ladies.

Soon as he was out of earshot, Gucci went in on Carla. "Bitch, you really is trippin, ain't you!"

"What you mean? I ain't did shit!" Carla put her shades over her eyes and sat back.

"Look, dummy, I could care less about yo dusty ass. You will never be my brother's girl in no way, shape or form. All I ask is if you wanna commit suicide, do it when I ain't around to witness the shit."

Gucci began collecting her items to leave when she saw three familiar silhouettes approaching from the horizon. Mia must've seen the figures too cause she took off running. Soon as she was in distance, she jumped on Gotti like she was a teenager and he was her favorite pop star. Her velocity almost knocked him off his feet. "Damn, shorty, you ain't miss me, did you?"

"You know I did."

Gutta and Money continued their trek through the sand, heading to Gucci and Carla. The stubborn females stared off in the distance, ignoring their presence. "Oh, so Mia the only one that miss her man?" Money stood directly in front of Gucci, blocking her view.

"Sorry, but I only miss people who miss me."

"So that's what it is ?"

"That's exactly what it is," Carla said, adding her two cents.

Gutta looked at Carla with a devious grin. "You riding the Gucci wave now, hunh?"

"I'm just saying she do got a point. You could've left me at home if you won't trynna kick it wit me."

Gutta looked at Gotti as he walked up with Mia. "Ay, bruh, we ain't getting no love."

"Oh yeah, you know I'm riding."

Mia looked at him like he was crazy. "Riding where?"

Money was the first to initiate the attack. He snatched Gucci off the beach chair, tossing her over his shoulder. "What you doin? Put me down!"

"Nah, fuck that. You so interested in the water, so I'mma help you out."

Gotti and Gutta both followed suit, grabbing their significant others. Gotti had Mia in a bear hug as she hit and scratched on his face. "No, Gotti, let me go! I ain't do shit!" Gutta seemed to be the smartest, grabbing Carla from the back so she couldn't hit his face.

"Ahhh!" the females screamed like they were actually being kidnapped.

Reaching the water, the guys walked as deep as they could before dumping the girls completely underwater. Gucci popped up first, wiping water from her face. "Nigga, you dirty. Word, that's messed up."

The men laughed hysterically. "That's probably what you needed to wash that stank attitude off," Gotti said.

"Oh yeah?" Gucci retaliated by jumping on Gotti as he floated on his back. She tried her best to keep him submerged underwater. Money quickly grabbed Carla, since she was the closest to him, body-slamming her, while Gutta did the same to Mia.

The men annihilated the women in their water war for the next hour. The playfulness was the perfect diversion from the stress they had been under lately.

* * *

As the sun went to sleep, Jamaica's nightlife became wide awake. The couples arrived at Ranks in a limousine chauffeured by the same dread-head who picked them up from the airport. The popular club was the island's hottest dance hall. The line outside was similar to Walmart when Tickle Me Elmo dropped. People were close enough to each other that their unintentional contact could've been misconstrued for sexual assaults. Damian had recommended this club during an earlier conversation. After being told that his associates would attend, he called ahead, informing security to provide the couples with all-access VIP service.

The limo pulled to a stop at the red carpet entrance with the driver rushing to open the back door. Whispers could be heard through the line as the passengers emerged. Money was first, stepping out dressed in a full blue True Religion outfit and blue Foam Posits sneakers. Holding his arm out, he helped Gucci step out, wearing a matching blue Michael Kors dress with Balenciaga red-bottom heels. They interlocked their arms as they strolled to the front door. Next was Gotti, who emerged from the limo dressed in a black and lime-green Trukfit outfit with all-black Jordan Dub Zeros and black Ray-Ban sunshades. On his arm was Mia in an all-black short catsuit with lime-green six-inch Gucci heels. Last was Gutta and Carla. Gutta donned a red Akoo outfit with Yeezy sneakers while Carla wore Seven jeans with a red Prada shirt and red Prada pumps. The entourage completely stole the spotlight as they walked the red carpet. They garnered so much attention, you would think they were members of the royal family. Many of the interested patrons snapped pictures or Googled who the stars could be.

Reaching the entrance, Money gave the security his name and was immediately allowed to bypass any type of security measure. The special treatment fascinated Carla, who constantly posted photos to Instagram or Facebook-Lived her experience. The club reeked of ganja while

Mad Cobra rocked the stage, performing his classic song "Flex." The native Jamaicans and sparse vacationists seemed to be in sync with each other as they dutty wined to the mellow rhythm. "*Flexa/Time to have sexa/Look how long you'll have the rude boy a sweat/Flexa.*"

"Ow shit, this my song." Carla sang along with the popular reggae artist. Pulling on Gutta's shirt, she led him to the dance floor. Usually he would contest but the shots of liquor and multiple blunts allowed him to be lured without resistance. Wrapping her arms around his neck, Carla grinded her body against his while two-stepping to the beat. Her head was laid against his shoulder as she spoke sweetly in his ear. "I'm sorry I'm not what you want, Gutta."

"What you talking bout, shorty?"

"I mean I know you be on them saddity bitches. That's all smart and classy but that's not me. I'm not like Gucci and Mia, and truthfully I don't think I wanna be."

Gutta chuckled. "Get out yo feelings, shorty. You all sentimental and shit."

"For real, Gutta. Dang, I'm being serious. I ain't neva did no shit like this before. I know it's only short-lived, but I just wanna thank you for choosing me when I know I ain't worth it." Carla was forcing back her tears.

Her words actually touched Gutta's heart. He remembered vividly the life of poverty and feelings of being worthless. A few years ago he would have never dreamed of a Jamaican vacation himself. Carla didn't know how much her words resonated in his heart. He stopped dancing and laid his palms on her cheeks. He held her head so that she would be looking directly in his eyes. "Real talk, Carla, I feel you. Just know that if you here, you here for a reason. Whether you or I know it, God chose this moment for us. So let's just enjoy it while it's here, aight?"

Carla smiled and laid her head back on Gutta's chest.

Back in the VIP, the other couples had ordered two bottles of Ace of Spades and were now hugged up, having isolated conversations amongst each other. Out of nowhere Damian entered, escorted by Chanta and two rugged-looking bodyguards. "Hey, star, wha ya do back here when de party out dere?"

"We just chillin right now."

"Ya no mine me join ya, no?"

"Nah, we good." Money sat up, giving the plug his attention.

"See, breadren, de next orda I double fa ya. I bless ya wit tree hundred keys instead of de one fifty."

Money quickly did the math in his head. Paying $10,000 a key, he could triple his net worth in a month. "Damn right, send that shit. I'mma still have the mill five for you on delivery."

"Ya bless ya breadren, no ya mus treasure de loyalty, star."

"My bros my equals, Damian. You know how I play it."

Damian raised his drink. With the clinking of glasses, the deal was sealed.

Suddenly, in the sea of partygoers, Gotti noticed a commotion was ensuing. In the crowd Gutta was dancing with Carla when they were approached by a tall Jamaican male. "Ey, Carla, I been lookin all ova for ya," Dink said after tapping her on the shoulder.

Panic was evident on her face as she stared back and forth between Gutta and Dink. "Wha…why?"

"We neva finish our conversation, gal."

Gutta looked at Carla with fire in his eyes before turning to Dink. "Bruh, I don't think shorty got no kick it for you, my nigga."

Dink frowned his face at Gutta's comment.

"Who ya boombaclot vacation boi talk to like that? Ya lack respect, boi."

Gutta felt his anger began to rise as he sized up the LeBron James-built Jamaican. His fist instantly clutched as he prepared to slay the Goliath of a man.

Before he could react, Gotti stepped up, throwing his arm around his brother's shoulder. "Everything good over here?" he asked.

Gutta continued grilling Dink. "Nah, bruh, dude think I disrespected him."

Knowing how quick his brother would go from zero to 100, Gotti tightened his grip around his shoulder. "Nah, everything good, my nigga." He placed a hundred-dollar bill on the bar before turning back to Dink. "That's my bad, gangsta. Go head and drink on me. We gone get out yo way." Gotti pulled his brother away and headed to the VIP. Carla followed behind like a lost puppy.

"Bruh, what you doing?" Gotti was displeased with Gutta.

"I was just letting dude know to back off shorty, but he got crazy out the mouth."

"Fam, you got the plug up there, my nigga, the plug. Looking, watching. You can bet he observing how you handle yourself out here. You think it's a good look to be out here fighting ova a bitch? You think he gone give a dumb ass nigga like that some bricks? Come on, fam, tighten up."

Gutta was embarrassed after analyzing the situation. "You right, bruh, I was buggin."

"Yeah, you was. You lucky I'm here to think for yo silly ass. We gotta get you back wit Ebony asap fore shorty turn you to another one."

"Oh, you trynna play me? I'll neva be another one." The brothers laughed.

Back at the VIP section, Gutta greeted Damian with a handshake. As he sat, Carla sat next to him, hanging her head like a disciplined toddler. "Gutta, Gutta, I'm sorry, bae."

"Don't sweat it, shorty, we good."

"No, it's just that—"

Gutta cut her off in mid-sentence. "Yo, don't fuck my night up. I said we good. Let that shit go."

Carla remained silent. Mia, who was now feeling the effects of her drinks, jumped on Gotti's lap. Grinding against his crotch, she provided him with a lap dance worthy of Magic City Mondays. The song "Limb by Limb" by Cutty Ranks reverberated throughout the building. Gotti was in a zone. With his shades down over his eyes, he puffed on a massive-sized blunt while drinking Ace of Spades straight from the bottle.

Gutta, who was also sipping from his personal bottle, noticed Carla was bobbing her head to the beat. "What you waiting on, shorty? I know you ain't gone let Mia show you up."

"Oh hell no, you know I do that shit forreal." She stuck out her tongue as she sat in Gutta's lap, twerking like she was trying for a Miley Cyrus video.

Damian, who was still sitting with Money, scrutinized the brothers' activities. With a grin on his face, he leaned over to Money. "Dat dere Gotti a special one, I tell ya. Rude boi like I. We do major tings in da future, the tree of us." Money looked at Gotti as he held his bottle in the air while Mia gyrated to the reggae anthem.

The VIP section was lit for the rest of the night. Gucci even joined in on the dance competition after seeing the fun her brothers were having. The festivities continued well into the wee hours of the morning before the vacationers stumbled to their villas and passed out.

The next afternoon Gotti woke up with an atrocious headache. Sitting up in the bed, he glanced over to find Mia, fully nude, sprawled out over the bed. Reaching over, he pulled the blanket over her body before heading to the kitchen. As he poured a tall glass of orange juice, he heard a strong vibrating sound on the counter. Hurriedly he went to answer as Tye's name flashed on the screen. "Yo."

"What's good, bruh? You still O.T.?"

"Yeah, we be back tomorrow, though."

"Yo. You might wanna cut that shit short."

"Why, what's up?"

"We caught this nigga Torn and 'em leaving Foots crib."

Gotti was hype. "Oh, y'all fixed his ass."

"Nah, man, I swear he had God on his side. Steve and Smoke got moked. I'm telling you, everything that could go wrong did. On some Murphy's law type shit."

"Fuck!" Gotti had to grind his teeth to control his anger.

"That ain't even the worst part, fam."

"My nigga, what could possibly be any worse?"

"After the shooting, Twelve ran in Foots spot and found Ms. Tina in there fucked up."

"My momma Ms. Tina? What you mean fucked up?"

"They say niggas did some foul shit to her. I ain't sure but she at Riverside right now."

"Aight, fam." Gotti was livid. Of course Ms. Tina had her flaws, but at the end of the day she was still his mother and family is family, regardless. Stressed to the point, his hand was shaking he called Gutta.

Groggily he answered on the fifth ring. "Yo."

"Bruh, pack up, we going home."

"When, now?"

"Yeah, my nigga, right now."

Chapter 11

Immediately after returning to the States, the three siblings made their way to Riverside

Regional Hospital. There Ms. Tina was being treated for injuries she sustained during the assault.

"We looking for Tina Walker," Gucci announced after approaching the reception desk.

The elder white lady who worked the area moved like a snail in a tortoise race. Placing

her huge bifocals over her eyes, she typed slowly on the decade-old computer. "I'm sorry but we

don't have a Trina Walker here."

"I said Tina...Tina Walker."

"Oh, Tina Walker. Ain't that something, my hearing seem to be getting worse every

day."

Gucci tried her best to maintain her composure. It took the lady nearly three long minutes

to come back with a room number. "Oh, here it go, room one-twelve. That's on the second floor

to the left...no...no, the right. You so beautiful. You look just like—"

"We got it, thanks." Gucci left the lady's words hanging in thin air.

The family stormed down the narrow hallways, relocating anything that was in their path.

Frantically they searched for room 112. "One-ten...one-eleven...one-twelve. Here, I found it."

Gucci was the first to enter. Ms. Tina lay on the hospital bed, passed out from the

anesthesia given to her during surgery. She was attached to more wires than a telephone pole and

had her legs placed in stirrups to keep them ajar. The sight of her was hard for any of her

children to digest. She had always been so outspoken and live that her current motionless state saddened them to the point of tears. They stood by her bedside, grief-stricken, when a tall, skinny white guy entered, wearing a long trench-type lab coat. "Excuse me, guys, may I ask who you all are?"

Gucci turned towards the doctor, wiping tears from her eyes. "Yeah, I'm Tierra Walker and these my brothers, Jaxavier and Jakahri. We her kids."

The doctor seemed satisfied with this explanation. Closing the door behind him, he walked further into the room. "Wonderful. Well, I'm Dr. Steward. I've been the one treating Ms. Walker since she was admitted here. Trying to make contact with any family members has been an uphill battle for us since she didn't have any emergency contacts on file. Honestly I just didn't know where to start."

"I'm sorry, we been out of town for the last couple days. We only recently found out and came soon as we could. Can you please tell us what happened?"

"First I would like to inform you that your mother is one strong individual and a blessed one at that. Of the five victims that night, she's the only one alive to talk about it."

Gotti grew impatient with the small talk. "Look, I don't mean no harm, but you ain't telling us shit. Why her legs open like that?" He pointed to the stirrups that supported Ms. Tina's legs.

"Of course. Mr. Walker, your mother was brutally assaulted and sexually penetrated. Whoever committed these heinous attacks filled her vaginal area with some type of hot cooking oil. The liquid scorched her internal organs and severely damaged her fallopian tubes, which we had to remove. Overall the surgery was a success."

The picture painted in Gotti's mind was far too vivid and painful for him to continue listening. In his mind he could hear the screams of his mother as she was literally burned from the inside out. "I'm out, yo, this some bullshit." He fled from the hospital room, leaving Gucci to continue the conversation with Dr. Steward.

"Pardon my brother, he's been through a lot lately. So is she gonna be okay?"

"I completely understand, this has to be hard for any child. Needless to say, when she awakes she will be in excruciating pain, which we will try to manage with medication until it subsides. The only long-term effect will be her inability to conceive children. Other than that she will live."

"Thank you, Doctor. Whatever this will cost, you just let us know, okay?"

"Will do, Ms. Walker. I'm just glad I was able to help." After shaking hands, the doctor exited the room.

Retaking her place beside Gutta, Gucci watched her sleeping mother carefully. As much as she despised Ms. Tina for her addiction, she hated to see her physically broken in the state she was in. The empathy she felt for her mother turned into rage in her heart. "Gutta, I need you to do something for me." She turned, facing her younger brother.

"What's up, sis?"

"You know I usually don't involve myself in y'all business. I don't condone nothing y'all do out there in them streets, but I do hear stories and I'm not green. All I ask that if you and your brother call yourselves your brother's keeper and y'all call yourself holding each other down, then this who you need to keep safe." She pointed to her mother. "This all our momma. Without her we nothing. Avenge her, Gutta…make sure this shit never happen again… Our pain need to be a two-way street, understand?"

Gutta looked back to his mother and shed a single solitary tear. Gucci's request was more than enough ammunition for him. Without a single word he stormed from the hospital room with the ambitions of a rider in his soul.

* * *

Gotti sat in the parking lot, seething over the vicious assault of his mother. The relatable words of Plies escaped his speakers. *"A goon to the streets but to my mom I'm still her baby/raised a street nigga by yourself you a helluva lady/the shit I'm doing ain't got nothing to do wit how you raise me/shit killin me to know I'm runnin my momma crazy."* Out of the corner of his eye he noticed Newport News police had formed a cypher around his car, pointing more nozzles at him than a wet t-shirt contest. "Freeze, don't move."

Refusing to be another Michael Brown news clip, he complied. He quickly stuck his arms out the window, allowing the officers to slap the cold cuffs on his wrists. Instantly he was dragged from the driver's seat of his vehicle and thrown in the back seat of theirs. As he stared out the window at the dramatic scene, he couldn't help but to dwell on how his life had spiraled out of control in the last week.

Detectives Brodey and Spider interrupted his view after approaching the back passenger window. By the smiles on their faces, one would suspect they had captured the leader of an Al-Queda terrorist group. "Mr. Walker, knew I would be seeing you again," said Detective Brodey. Gotti sat silently, gaze colder than Icebreakers chewing gum. "Oh, you ain't got nothing to say, hunh? You still wanna fuck my daughter? Too bad you can't get pussy on death row."

The detectives slammed the car door, leaving Gotti to ride to Newport News city jail, charged with the first-degree murder of Marcus Knight.

* * *

Newport News city jail bullpen was the filthiest place Gotti had ever been. On the wall was three-day-old dinner from where somebody had slung their tray after their bond was denied. Beside that was the urine of a drunk who just couldn't hold his bladder any longer. After being searched, photographed, and fingerprinted, Gotti was tossed in along with the rest of the city's criminal element.

Taking a seat on the hard metal bench, he dropped his face in his hands, stewing in his misery. Never in a million years had he thought that karma would reach backwards and molest his mother. Not even David Blaine could escape the torment he felt over her repulsive predicament. Marathon thoughts of "if" raced through his brain. If his adolescent rage hadn't been released upon Marco, then his mother's health would have never been jeopardized and he wouldn't be sitting in the spot he was currently.

A familiar voice called his name, snatching him from his thoughts and gaining his attention. "Young Gotti!" Gotti raised his head to see Thugga approaching him from the other side of the bullpen. "What's cracken, ace."

"What's good, fam." Gotti extended his hand to dap the rapper up. Thugga was one of the artists on Money's label back in the day. Gotti had not seen him since his first visit to the River Walk studio when Jazz-o was laying his track. "Where you disappeared to, bruh?" Gotti questioned as Thugga took a seat beside him.

"Man, I had to leave Hollywood and get back to the trenches."

"I can dig it, fam."

"You one nigga I ain't think I was gone run into in this bitch, though. What's good?"

"Ain't nothing good, fam. Crackers trynna railroad me like they did O.J."

"That shit crazy, ace."

Gotti scrutinized Thugga's forest-green jumpsuit. "I definitely can ask you the same shit, though."

"I'm going to my preliminary right now. Donnie Brasco ass nigga put me on to a lick, then try to drop on me. But you know me, solid as a block of ice."

Air suddenly released from the metal door leading to the lockup area. The pair watched as a group of inmates were escorted in. "Damn. What's cracken, cuz?" A medium-built brown-skinned dude approached Thugga.

"What's cracken?" The two saluted each other with a special handshake, locking the letter "C" at the end. Gotti analyzed the gangbangers' movement, deciphering whether he would embrace his presence or not.

"Noon, this my nigga Gotti… Gotti, this the homie Noon."

"What's cracken?" Noon greeted Gotti. Gotti simply nodded in return.

Noon turned his attention back to Thugga. "What you doing in here, cuz?"

"Preliminary. This shit ain't bout nothing, though."

"Word. You know I was posed to go home off this J-love bid, but these people trynna hit me wit a street charge for wreaking wit this bitch ass C.O."

"Damn, ace."

"Walker!"

Gotti rose as his name was announced by Deputy Brooks. "Yo."

"Come on, the magistrate ready for you."

The gate opened so the female deputy could escort Gotti. They walked through a set of metal doors into an area outside a small courtroom. Deputy Brooks stood to the side, waiting for the magistrate to finish with the suspects in front of Gotti. Her wide hips and voluptuous backside held the gaze of every male in her general vicinity. Gotti couldn't help but stare as she seemed to intentionally make sure his view of her was unobstructed the entire time.

Five minutes later his name was finally called. Brooks led him in. "Mr. Jaxavier Walker, I see here you have been charged with the first degree murder of a Mr. Marcus Knight as well as use of a firearm in commission of a felony. Your record shows you have a number of prior non-processed or dismissed charges. That, along with the severity of your current charges, does not allow me to grant you a bond at this time." Gotti remained expressionless, knowing full well he wouldn't receive a bond the moment they slapped the cuffs on his wrist. "Furthermore, you will be scheduled a formal arraignment tomorrow at ten o'clock, at which you will be presented a lawyer to assist you with your case. Are there any questions I could answer for you?"

"Nah."

"Great. Well, at this time you will be turned back over to Newport News city sheriff's office."

Gotti gingerly slid out of the courtroom, grimacing from the metal cuffs that dug into the back of his ankles. "Yo, Dep, you gotta loosen these shits up."

"Why you ain't been told me they was too tight?"

"I was good till they started to draw blood from a nigga."

Deputy Brooks laughed at Gotti's wisecracks. Squatting in her Nicki Minaj stance, she loosened the shackles. "Good look, shorty."

Back in the bullpen Thugga and Noon had been indulging in a tense conversation. Gotti noticed the mood as soon as he was inserted back with the rest of the riff-raff. "Yo, what's good?" he asked.

"Ain't shit. What they talking bout in there?"

"You know they tied me to the F150, something small to a giant, though."

"I already know, they dragging me too. I'm trynna hurry up in this courtroom and see what's up."

"Walker, phone call!" Deputy Brooks opened the gate for Gotti to receive his one free call.

Ring...Ring. "Hello."

"Yo, Mia, what's good, gorgeous?"

"Gotti? Why you calling from this weird number?"

"I'm in jail, bae. They got me down at Newport News, charged with murder."

Mia's gasp was heart-wrenching. "Oh my God, Gotti! Murder!"

"Don't sweat it, I'm good. Just call Gutta and my lawyer, Callahan. Tell Gutta what's up and tell the lawyer he need to be at my arraignment tomorrow." Through an awkward silence, Gotti could hear Mia's sobs. "Yo, Mia, what's up?"

"I'm...I'm here. I'mma do it."

"Come on, bae, don't cry. I need you to be strong right now."

Mia could not suppress her emotions. "It hurt, Gotti! I can't do this! I can't lose you! I love you too much!" She was all-out bawling now.

"I'm not going nowhere, love. Just be tough for me. You my soldier, Mia. How our song go? When all odds against me, I need someone to come get me. I need what, Mia?" Through her tears she was barely able to speak, so he asked again. "What I need, Mia?"

"A na... A Navy SEAL. I'mma be your Navy SEAL, bae. I got you, that's law."

Gotti smiled at his queen's use of his vocabulary. "Already then." Gotti ended the call, feeling like Jesus when he walked on water. With Mia in his corner, there was no way he would drown. Never before had he contemplated settling down with one woman, but after all Mia had been through with him, he would really have to put some serious thought into putting a ring on it.

Deputy Brooks patted him down before reinserting him into the bullpen. He noticed the tension in the air had turned toxic soon as the bars were closed behind him. Thugga was posted on one side of the room with Noon on the opposing side. The two were sizing each other up like the weigh-in at a Floyd Mayweather/Conor McGregor prize fight. Before he could interpret what was about to happen, Noon charged him, swinging a makeshift knife at Gotti's face like Brad Pitt in the movie *Troy*. Dodging the assailant's attack, Gotti ducked, causing the sharp steel instrument to miss, striking the concrete wall behind him. Imitating a WWE wrestler, Gotti attached his body to Noon's, body-slamming him to the ground. His weapon dropped from his hand and slid halfway across the room. Unfortunately Noon didn't surrender. Hopping up swiftly, he caught Gotti with a one-two combo that dazed him to the point of momentary vision loss.

Thugga stood off, evaluating his position. It was hard for him to decide between his homie or his friend. Invading the one-on-one bout, he threw his weight into a right hook that stunned Noon into submission. The jail's sheriffs sufficiently engulfed the bullpen from all angles, applying pressure to the necks and wrists of all three participants.

Gotti was furious after being tossed in the isolation cell in the lockup area. The audacity of Noon to ambush him was a direct insult to his character.

"Yo, Gotti!" Thugga was three cells down from him.

"Yo."

"You good down there, my nigga?"

"Always, fam. What's up wit yo homie, though?"

"Man, he was talking some shit bout riding for his nigga Torn. I told him it was dead cause it have nothing to do wit Crip but dude stupid."

"Yeah. Don't trip. I'mma learn his lil young ass real quick though."

"I already know what time it is, Gotti. Just cause dude cuz don't mean he family, my nigga."

"Undastood."

There was a pause in their conversation as Gotti reflected on his new friend's actions. He respected the gangster's choice to do what was right instead of what was easy. "Thugga, what happened to you anyway, fam? Jazz-o out touring right now and Doc just dropped a national mixtape. You had next, my nigga, why you dip?"

"Them niggas had time to waste and I had a family to feed."

"Why you just ain't tell Money? I know he would've threw you something."

"You know I did. When I did he threw me some lame ass excuse bout niggas that don't work don't deserve a portion, but he won't trynna give me a seat at the table. He just wanted a nigga to rap like we was his lil toys or some shit."

"Hold up, I can't go for that, bruh. Money put me on when I ain't have nothing. I know he ain't carry it like that."

"Don't get me wrong, he toss me some crumbs too, but what's that. I'll jack a nigga fore I let him bird feed me. That's just what it is."

Gotti was baffled by Thugga's portrayal of the man who had just showed him Jamaica for the first time in his life. "Look, bruh, we just gone end this conversation."

"I feel you, Gotti. I already know how you love yo brothers. Just remember every snake don't shed his skin."

* * *

"*I been going through some thangs/don't nobody understand me, man /I wanna ride candy, man/I been going through some thangs/hopin my niggas stay the same but they always change/I been going through some thangs.*" Gutta and Money cruised Mercury Boulevard, listening to Lil Boosie, when Gutta felt his phone vibrate in his lap. "Yo, turn that down right quick, this Mia." Money pressed the mute button on his sound system. "Yo, Mia, what's up."

"Gotti got locked up!"

Gutta's heart dropped like cement blocks in a plastic pool. "Locked up for what?"

"He said they charged him wit murder. He in the Newport News city right now."

"Damn, Gotti! Did you call Callahan yet?"

"Nah, I was bout to do that now."

"Aight, call him and tell him call me when he find out what's up."

"Kay."

Gutta dropped the phone on the car's floor as his agony set in. From Ebony to Gotti, it seemed karma had his loved ones solely in her crosshairs. No matter how swift they were, it was just impossible to escape.

Overhearing the conversation, Money took a glimpse into the passenger seat to find Gutta with his eyes closed and his head pressed firmly against the headrest. "What's up, bruh? What good wit Mia?"

"Man, this nigga Gotti got booked, fam."

The revelation threatened to leave Money speechless. "Damn."

"Yeah, damn is right."

"What he locked for?"

"Mia said a body but she ain't call the lawyer yet so she don't got no details."

"You know you might have to hold shit down dolo till he come up from under that joint."

"I already know. I can't believe this shit though." Gutta punched the dashboard.

"It's gone be aight, bruh. Look, reach in the back seat and grab that bag for me."

Gutta reached back, retrieving the Wilson sports bag. "What's this?"

"That's twenty-five bricks right there."

"Twenty-five! Damn, who these going to?"

"That's you right there. You gone have to grind twice as hard, but this city yours, my nigga, you just gotta take it."

"I ain't got the bread for twenty-five right now, especially wit Gotti gone."

"That shit ain't bout nothing, Gutta. You talkin to me bout some bread. Just throw me two hundred thousand now and two hundred thousand when you done."

After doing the math in his head, Gutta was pleased with the discounted price. "That's love, fam, word."

"Nah, Gutta. Love is love, loyalty is everything."

Chapter 12

Two months had passed since Gotti was indicted for Marco's murder. Since then Gutta hit the air flying with the advancement of bricks by Money. In no time he conquered the entire downtown drug market. His team flipped birds like Simone Biles in gymnastics practice. The incarceration of his brother gave him free rein to make many rash decisions without any resistance whatsoever. His most notorious decision was the one to intrude on any territory he decided he could get some money on. Those decisions made him a very hated and feared man. He modified the concept of love and fear given to him so long ago into simply fear. His blueprint was to rule the city with an iron fist.

He, Tye, and M.A. arrived at the Hampton Coliseum in his 2013 eggshell-white Bentley Azure convertible. The cabriolet seat covering with embroidered Bentley motif, 20-inch chrome wheels, and Alpine premium high-end sound system displayed the extravagance of the vehicle to everybody with eyes to see. Tonight was the kickoff of Cash Money's reunion tour. Lil Wayne, B.G., Juvenile, Turk, and Baby were scheduled to appear, enticing the entire Tidewater area to attend the star-studded event. Money invited the whole squad, supplying his top earners with scarce backstage passes. Gutta, being his usual overbearing self, commandeered enough passes to grant his entire entourage access.

Jazz-o, who was scheduled to open for the legendary rappers, was in a dressing room along with Money, Dyco, Q, and Doc. Gutta and his team entered and exchanged salutations with the room's occupants. Everybody had pulled out their best gear for the show. Gutta, being the most ostentatious, elevated the bar tremendously. In a full Prada outfit equipped with two gold and diamond Jesus face chains, flawless diamond stud earrings, and a gold and diamond watch, he looked like he was there to perform rather than watch the concert.

Money approached the gang, smoking on a blunt of exotic weed. "What's up, Gutta."

The two friends embraced. "What's good?"

"Ain't shit. You holla at Gotti?"

"Who?"

"Gotti, yo brother."

"Oh, nah." Gutta had been ingesting molly for the last 48 hours straight. The drugs had him completely fried and more egotistical than he usually was.

The room's door opened. The concert manager stuck her head in and was quickly overcome by the thick clouds of marijuana smoke. With her shirt held over her nose, she informed Jazz that he had five minutes to perform. The room erupted in applause. "You ready, fam?" Money dapped up his young artist.

"Been ready."

Gutta and his clique made their way to the crowd. Even though they could watch the show from backstage, they wanted to feel the energy of the multitude of people and party with the slew of desirable females.

Three hours later the night was still invigorated with the mass of concertgoers pouring into the Coliseum's parking lot. "Yo, that shit was dumb lit." M.A. was still full of vim.

"Damn right, B.G. thuggin forreal." Tye slurred his words. He was inebriated from consuming numerous shots of Cîroc the entire show.

Money and Gutta's entire gang congregated and paraded through the parking lot. From the distance Gutta heard his name shouted from across the lot. Scanning the area, he noticed Carla approaching, scantily clad in a pair of denim booty shorts, a denim tube top, and Jimmy Choo high heel shoes. "Hey, beau!" She jumped on Gutta, wrapping her arms around his neck.

He quickly hit her with the Heisman stiff arm, making sure she wouldn't try to put her lips anywhere near his face. "What's up, yo."

"Damn, why you ain't been answering my calls?"

"I been busy. Why?"

"I just wanted to spend some time wit you, that's all."

"Time is money, shorty, and I ain't got neither one to waste."

"Damn, nigga, you act like I ain't got no money. I'm dancing in K.O.D. every other weekend now."

"So?"

"So come spend the night wit me. I'll pay for everything. Plus I got some new moves you might wanna see." Carla bit her bottom lip.

Gutta rationalized his decision. Carla did look like she had added a little weight in all the right places, plus she always had some of the better sex he had ever had. "Aight, get a room and I'll swing through before the night over. Go head and have that shit fresh for me too."

Carla was overjoyed. "Of course. You know I'mma be right for you."

Gutta felt a tap on his shoulder that momentarily startled him. "Oh shit." It hit him like a ton of bricks to turn and see Ebony standing there, beaming.

"Why you look like you seen a angel, Gutta? Speechless, hunh?"

"Damn, shorty, when you came back?"

"I woke up bout a month ago, but you woulda knew that if you gave a fuck. Where you been at, Gutta?"

"I been around, damn."

His response stunned Ebony. "Around? I been trynna find you for the longest. You out this bitch like Waldo and you talking bout you been around. Are you serious?"

"What you think I'm stupid, yo? Do I look like the Tin Man or some shit? Got me stressin ova yo thot ass when you got a baby by Marco. Bitch, you got me bent."

Gutta's words stung Ebony's ears. "Marco! I just took a bullet for yo ass and you trippin bout who my babydaddy is. Really, Gutta! Nah, you got me bent, bitch!"

Gutta chuckled. "Whateva, Ebony. I'mma holla at you." He turned to Carla, who was scrutinizing the spectacle like it was Jerry Springer's 3,000th episode. "Get the room. I'mma hit you up in a lil bit."

"Kay, bae." She looked at Ebony and smiled before trotting off.

Tears poured from Ebony's eyes like alcohol from a tilted wine keg. "You dirty, Gutta. How you gone play me like this after all I been through? I been in yo corner from day one! Yo lover! … Yo friend! … Yo everything! … From day one! When you ain't have shit, I was there! You a fuckin dog, my nigga, forreal."

"A friend of my enemy could never be my friend, Ebony. I learned that a long time ago." Pivoting, Gutta walked away, leaving Ebony there frozen like Lake Michigan in December.

* * *

Gutta, Tye, and M.A. arrived at the Waffle House on Mercury Boulevard in Gutta's Bentley directly behind Money, Dyco, and Q in Money's black Mercedes Benz truck. The parking lot was popping with a congregation of partygoers. Posted by a silver Mercedes Benz CLS was Lump, Hotboy, and K.T. A group of promiscuous females was flirting with the 21st Street hustlers, attempting to find their next baby daddy.

"Yo, Gutta." Lump spotted the plug from a distance and started his approach.

"What's up, yo?" Gutta stopped while his gang proceeded to the restaurant.

"You been aight, fam? I been trynna holla at chu for bout two weeks now."

"Yeah, I ain't get the memo."

Lump was thrown off by Gutta's smug comment. Brushing it off, he continued, "When you gone come scoop this seventy-five grand I got for you? Shit been like the Sahara out the hood."

"I'm not."

"Fuck you mean you not?"

"I'm not. Don't play yoself, my nigga. You know I don't fuck wit y'all. That's Gotti and Gotti ain't here. So pardon me." Gutta showed Lump his back as he rejoined his clique inside the restaurant.

Lump was stewing. He wanted so bad to teach the smartmouthed hustler a lesson but decided against it. Killing Gutta is something Gotti would never have understanding for, and to Gotti he would always remain loyal. Shaking his head, he went back to his CLS and exited the parking lot.

The Waffle House held the aroma of fried bacon and maple syrup. Every customer had just left the concert, giving the restaurant the appearance of an after-hours social gathering. Newport News police even assigned two uniformed officers to maintain order. "Yo, it's no way we waiting for a table," Dyco said.

"Let me go talk to the manager right fast." Money went to the register while the others stood by the entrance.

Gutta leaned against the old-school jukebox, fading from all the molly and marijuana. Suddenly he heard his name shouted across the room. He dropped his head in irritation. Calling his name seemed like the theme for the night. Everywhere he went it was Gutta this or Gutta that. Truthfully he was fed up and on the verge of calling it a night and laying up with Carla. Looking to the back of the restaurant, his blood steamed to see Torn standing in the aisle, arms extended like Leonardo DiCaprio in the *Titanic* movie. "What's up, gangsta."

Gutta's disdain for his enemy was magnetic. Two quick steps later he was wrapped up by Money and Dyco. "Not here, Gutta. You gotta let him live right now." Money was talking in his ear.

"Let him live! You got me fucked up, get the fuck off me."

"Nah, fam, be smart, twelve right there."

Gutta glimpsed at the cops who were now observing the confrontation with their hands firmly pressed against their holsters. Livid, he stormed out the door without even looking back in Torn's direction. It pained him to humble himself in the midst of his adversaries.

Riding on the interstate after dropping his team off on 36th Street, he single-mindedly plotted his vengeance. The hellish grin and words of Torn reverberated through his brain.

Snapping him out of his thoughts, his phone shook in his lap. The screen said unknown. He turned the volume down on his music before answering. "Yo, who dis?"

"Torn at the Red Roof Inn."

"What? Who dis?"

"Room two-two-four." The phone went dead.

His heart pace increased. His mind immediately thought that this would be a set-up. The words of the unknown caller incited a charge that was sure to lead him either to prison or the grave. As he raced to the Red Roof Inn, he figured either one would be a welcomed experience as long as Torn's existence expired first.

Parking his car at the Super Eight hotel, Gutta jogged across the highway to the Red Roof Inn. A white SUV was just leaving as he entered the parking lot. He had taken all his jewelry off and put on an all-black hoodie he had in his trunk. He didn't bother to bring backup. To him anybody else would only be in the way. On top of that, if it was a set-up, he wouldn't be responsible for anyone of his soldiers' demise. This was just one journey he would take by himself.

He tucked his Mac-10 under his shirt as he made his way up the steps to the second floor of the hotel. The entire area was quiet. He noticed the light on room 224 was on and the blinds were closed. He attempted to slow his breathing as he placed his ear to the door, listening for sounds. Inside he heard a female voice and at least one male voice. This was all he needed to confirm that his invasion would be justified. He pulled his Mac from under his shirt, making sure everything was functional.

His first idea was to knock on the door and then bumrush when somebody answered. Quickly he scratched that one. It wouldn't be smart at all to alert his prey of his presence. So with both hands gripping the Mac, he stepped back and booted the door as hard as he could. "You betta not fuckin move!"

Inside was one male and one female, fully nude. On the TV a Pinky porno tape was playing. Carla scrambled to pull the blanket over her bare body, leaving the male with nothing to cover his member. He still had the condom on. "Yo, what's up? What's all this?" His fear caused him to break out in cold sweats.

"Where the fuck Torn at?"

"Torn?"

"Real talk, don't play wit me. Where Torn at?"

"I don't know Torn."

"Oh, you don't." Gutta had already recognized the guy's face from the Waffle House. With his gun still aimed at the naked male, he walked over to the bed and snatched Carla by her hair, dragging her to the floor. She screamed for her life as her bodacious breasts bounced in every direction.

Standing over her, Gutta pressed the gun to the top of her cranium. "Gutta, please! I'm sorry."

"Shut up, bitch! Where Torn at?"

"Yo, chill, I don't know Torn!" the male said.

Carla was crying hysterically. Snot was dripping from her nose as she thought of how tragic the situation could turn out. "Wait! Wait! Torn just left," she shouted.

"Shut the fuck up, Carla!"

"Fuck you, Tone, I'm not dying for yo punk ass cousin. Like I said, Torn just left in a white SUV."

"Fuck!" Gutta was disappointed in himself. He just let his target ride right past him. "Why you lie to me, fam? I thought you ain't know Torn."

"I was scared, my nigga. I can call him for you right now, though." Tone realized he didn't have a leg to stand on.

"Too late, you had yo chance." Aiming the Mac at Tone's chest, Gutta pulled the trigger, releasing five rapid shots into the guy's frame.

"Ahhhh!" Carla was panicking. She used her hands to cover her eyes from the bullet-riddled corpse in front of her.

Gutta let her hair go. Quickly she scurried across the floor, placing her back to the dresser. "Please! Please! Don't kill me, Gutta, I got kids." She saw her pleas were making him hesitate, so she continued. "I love you, baby. I swear I do. I just fucked up."

Gutta saw the desperation on her face. She was petrified at the prospect of death. "Damn, shorty!" She stared down the barrel of the gun as Gutta aimed it at her forehead. Fortunately she didn't see the bullet empty the chamber. Blood oozed from the hole in her head as she died with her eyes open.

Gutta strolled out the front door, using his shirt to pull it closed. After trotting back across the street, he entered the car and removed his hoodie. Wiping the sweat from his face, he called Gucci. "Hello," she answered groggily.

"Yo, I'm bout to crash at yo shit tonight. Unlock the door."

"Aight. Everything good, bruh?"

"Yeah, sis, everything good."

* * *

Gotti was assigned to three-one pod in Hampton Roads regional jail. His high-profile case got him transferred there due to Newport News jail's inability to guarantee security. The regional jail in Portsmouth, Virginia, was where different localities sent their inmates for various reasons such as overcrowding, escape risk, nuisance complaints, etc. Newport News, Hampton, Norfolk, and Portsmouth all contracted the jail to house their inmates.

Gotti had just come back from the inside basketball court, playing a game of three on three. While waiting for his turn in the shower, he decided to call Lump.

Ring... Ring... Ring. "Yo."

"You have a collect call from Gotti, an inmate at Hampton Roads regional jail. To accept, please dial 'zero' now." *Beep!* "Your call is being connected."

"Yo."

"What's good, Gotti?"

"Ain't shit, fam, what's good wit you?"

"I'm Gucci, my nigga. Why you ain't been hit me up?"

"I ain't talking bout shit forreal. These people keep pushing my date back, got me stressing badder than a muthafucka."

"I feel you, bruh. Shit just a minor setback for a major comeback though. You gotta hold yo head."

"I already know."

"Yeah, you tough, nigga, stop bitchin."

"Fuck you." The duo laughed. The conversation was starting to cheer Gotti up. "What's good on yo end, though?"

"I been in the way lately, bruh, to keep it a band wit you."

"How?"

"Yo brother Gutta been feeling hisself like Beyoncé and Nicki."

Gotti pulled the phone back from his ear and looked at it, trying to understand if he was hearing Lump correct. "What you mean by that?"

"Dude stop putting on for niggas. Then when I see him and ask him bout it, he try to let his nuts hang on me."

"Real shit?"

"Yeah, real shit. The only reason I ain't serve him shots like a bartender was outta respect for you."

"If that's what it is, then I appreciate you, bruh. Word."

"You already know. I can't be the one to make Ms. Tina grieve, that's mama forreal."

"So what you doing out there?"

"Nothing major. I had to holla at Money nigga Q the other day but that ain't even close to what I was doing. I might just let that shit go for a while. Plus bruh got all my niggas scared to eat. He run shit from Forty-First to Ninth."

"Damn, bruh moving reckless like that?"

"Yeah. For a second I thought you stamped it."

"Nah, I ain't know none of that, but bruh bout to hear bout it, real talk."

"Word. Just get wit me, fam, and remember to keep yo head up."

"Love you, my nigga."

"Already."

Gotti terminated that call and dialed Gutta's number without a moment's hesitation. The phone rang continuously about six times before the operator kicked in. Gotti hit the receiver, rapidly dialing his brother's number again.

"Yo, Gotti, I had next." DJ, a minute flunky from Norfolk, stood ice-grilling like Gotti had kicked his dog.

"What?"

"I'm saying I had called next on that phone, few."

"Nigga, fuck you. Holla at me when I'm done."

Gotti proceeded with his call. This time Gutta answered on the second ring. "Yo." The operator went through its automatic routine. "Damn, my fault, bruh. I left my phone in the kitchen."

"Look, shit coming cross my ears and I ain't feeling it."

"What you talking bout now, Gotti?"

"You ain't seen my nigga Lump lately?"

"Nah, I ain't checking for him neither."

"What? ... You know he my brother like my mother son. Carrying him like carrying me. So what's up?"

"I ain't wit that shit, Gotti, you know that. That's just what it is right now."

"So my word ain't law, that's what you sayin?"

"I guess not. Laws change every day."

"You being dumb right now, bruh."

"Man, call it what you want. I'm out here dolo so I'm doing me."

"The sun don't always shine in the ghetto, Gutta, remember that."

"Fuck it. It only rain in my hood anyway."

Gotti ended the call, feeling like Abel and Gutta was his Cain.

* * *

Gutta was saddened by his brother's disapproval. Since a child he loved and respected Gotti. Chastisement was just something that didn't sit well with him. Not in the mood for any attention, Gutta pulled into the Harpoon Larry's parking lot in his silver Diamante. He usually used the factory car for drop-offs and pick-ups. Today its purpose was to make him as inconspicuous as possible.

Harpoon Larry's was a seafood restaurant on Mercury Boulevard where white society members went to loosen their ties and let their hair down. The purpose of his visit was to meet with two young ladies who started a national trend with their S.S. Clothing line. S.S. is an abbreviation for street sacrifices. The wardrobe started a major online movement when Remy Ma appeared in concert with a shirt featuring Lauryn Hill smiling in her prison jumpsuit. High-fashion designers and fashion critics immediately shunned the line, detesting what it meant for black Americans. Gutta was contacted by a mutual female friend who persuaded him that investing in the company would be the perfect down payment on his future. Thinking of the near $3 million he kept in a self-storage rental facility, he reasoned the line would be the perfect way to launder his drug money.

Arriving fifteen minutes late, he walked in to see two brown-skinned females seated at a booth in the corner. "I hope I'm the one y'all waiting for," he said, approaching the ladies.

"I hope so too. I'm Latoi and this my sister Nina," the older of the two greeted Gotti, extending her hand for him to shake.

Latoi and Nina Ross were sisters from Newport News, Va. Growing up admiring the fashions of movie stars and music artists, they dreamed of creating something that would be showcased on the red carpet of the Met Gala. After receiving over two million Twitter followers, the spark was lit to elevate S.S. Clothing beyond their wildest imaginations.

Gutta took a seat in the booth opposite the sisters. "So y'all the ones killin the game, hunh?"

"Nah, the game been dead. We here to put it back on life support."

"I can dig it. So let me hear y'all vision."

"Well, we already took a major step in the right direction with the publicity Remy Ma receiving. Our plan is to continue in that lane with different prints of our incarcerated black queens and kings." Nina passed Gutta a three-ring binder. "In there you will see numerous photos and jail mugshots we plan to use as our next graphics."

Gutta opened the book to see mugshots of Assata Shakur, Remy Ma, Lil Kim, Winnie Mandela, and a slew of other African American prisoners. Fairly impressed, he nodded his head, giving his approval. Latoi then passed him another binder. "In this one is our designs to extend our line to jeans, shoes, belts, and jewelry accessories."

Gutta was blown away by the females' presentation. They really created a product he could get behind. It was easy to visualize the whole world wearing the clothing. "Okay, that shit poppin, but let's talk numbers. Why you need my investment if you already getting promoted by mainstream rappers?"

"See, that's the dilemma. We basically getting blackballed by the fashion industry. No factory in America willing to produce enough of our product to supply our customers, so basically we got two options. Option number one is go foreign, which we really not trynna do."

"Why not?"

"We just feel it's too many of our brothers and sisters here that need a job for us to provide jobs for some Chinese muthafuckas we don't even know."

"Word, I feel that. So what's option two?"

"We build our own factory. That's where you come in. Every dollar you give will be used to literally build a full-functioning factory from the ground up."

"How much you need?"

The sisters looked at each other. "Well, all of it. We need you to pay for everything. Maybe half a mill to a million to start with."

This was usually where the designers lost a majority of their potential investors, so you could imagine the shock when Gutta opened his mouth to speak. "Bet, I'm wit it. Draw up a contract and have it presented to me by the end of the week. I'll go over it wit my lawyer and make any amendments I deem necessary, but other than that, I'm locked in."

The sisters shrieked with excitement. "Really? Oh my God! Oh my God! We did it!" The entire restaurant viewed the outburst, wondering what could make the ladies so cheerful.

Gutta rose from his booth. "Congratulations. Make sure I get that contract."

"Definitely." He extended his hand to seal the deal with a handshake. "No fuckin way." Both sisters jumped on Gutta, squeezing his neck in a joyful embrace.

"Damn, shorty, don't kill me before I sign the check." The designers laughed.

Gutta exited the building and entered his Diamante, feeling like one of the CEOs on *Undercover Boss*. His entire life had been filled with negativity. Finally doing something positive was his biggest accomplishment to date and he loved it.

Chapter 13

Torn stood in the River Walk apartment with the intentions of purchasing five bricks of cocaine from the largest distributer in the city. He brought Bud along for protection while Fatts supervised operations in their newly acquired Aqueduct apartments. The meeting was set up by Arab, whose baby mother recently moved to the uptown neighborhood. Seeing the untapped potential, Arab gave Torn the blueprint that Money laid out for all of his business associates to maximize their income. After being informed of Arab's methodical activities, Money immediately rejected the notion, but Arab was relentless. In his persuasion attempts, he convinced Money that he should remove himself from the brothers' war and get money. That was over a month ago. Torn's willingness to pay $27,000 a brick was enough for Money to finally consent.

"How business going uptown, Torn?" Money sat at the apartment's kitchen table, surrounded by his closest confidants and enforcers. Dyco, Q, and Arab all took positions around the room.

"Shit been good, thanks to you."

"That's what's up. Look, I ain't even gone waste none of your time. It's a reason why I asked to see you today."

"Oh yeah, and why is that?"

"This situation with you, Gotti, and Gutta beginning to keep me up at night, and I like to sleep. Simply put, the whole shit out of control. It ain't gone bring nobody back, and truthfully it's bad for business."

Torn shrugged his shoulders. "You know what it is, Money. That shit only gone end when I see my brother again."

"Listen to me closely. Something need to happen asap, cause if this shit come to my doorstep, then it become my problem, dig it?"

"Like a shovel."

"Go head, Arab, get 'em straight. I'mma slide to the studio right quick."

"Aight."

The goons accompanied their leader from the apartment. Arab went to the back room, emerging with five kilos. Torn pulled bundles of cash from the Goyard tote bag, stacking $135,000 on the glass table. "I ain't gotta count that shit, do I?" Arab joked.

"That's on you but I damn sho don't got all day to wait."

"I'm fucking wit you. But real talk, one way or the other, you gotta end that beef. A body without a head should be easily toppled."

Torn thought a second on Arab's riddle. Quickly he reasoned he was being told to topple Gutta while Gotti was locked, which was exactly what he planned to do.

* * *

Gutta had just left his lawyer's office, reviewing the contract drawn up by his S.S. Clothing business partners. The document was drafted exceptionally well with only a few amendments to be put in place, the main one being the nondisclosure agreement allowing the females to refuse revealing investors without a warrant being produced. After the murder of

Carla and Tone, he thought he would be doomed to dwell in hell for the rest of his life. As he

navigated his way up Jefferson Boulevard with the sun shining and a signed contract in his glove

box, he could only hope that maybe things would look up for him after all. For days now he had

concealed his business endeavors from everybody, not wanting to jinx anything that wasn't

already guaranteed. Now that everything was finalized, he was anxious to boast on his

accomplishments.

Making a right into the River Walk parking lot, he was met head-on by a Land Rover

exiting on the wrong side. Abruptly hitting the brakes, he stopped just in time to avoid a

collision. His anger rose. Ready to curse the reckless driver out, he looked through the Rover's

front windshield at his archenemy. He was astonished. "Bitch muthafucka." Reaching under his

seat, he gripped the handle of his brand new .380. In a murderous rage, he jumped from the car,

pumping slug after slug into the front window, attempting to decapitate his targets.

The first shot struck Bud in his collarbone, collapsing him over the armrest. Torn ducked,

feeling like a target on PlayStation's Metal Gear Solid. Pressing the gas pedal to the floor, he

crashed into Gutta's Diamante, driving the car backwards. Gutta trained his weapon at the Land

Rover, sending the truck more bullets than a gun shop. *Click.* The gun's chamber locked. "Shit."

He was furious, realizing that his backup clip was in the car.

Sirens were approaching quickly. All movement in the neighborhood ceased. Most of the

residents were in their houses, curled under tables like it was an earthquake drill. Even though

Gutta was unsatisfied, he just had to hope he had executed his mission properly. He took off for

the closest apartment Money used as one of his distribution spots.

Arab was hurrying to stash the drugs before the police flooded the projects. Suddenly at the front door he heard three knocks, followed by a brief pause, then three more knocks. Detecting the rhythm, he unlocked and opened the door. Gutta bumrushed the apartment, nearly knocking him off his feet. "Yo, where the fuck Money at?"

Arab slammed the door shut. "First off, slow the fuck down. You bustin in here like the alphabet boys or some shit."

"What? Fuck all that, where Money at?"

"He ain't in my Jordans. Why?"

"Man, you playing and Torn was just out here trynna lay on me."

"What you do, Gutta?"

"You know what I did. I fixed his ass like a flat tire, that's what I did."

"I told Money bout fuckin wit y'all lil niggas. You fuckin the bread up. Torn just spent over a hundred grand wit niggas."

Gutta felt betrayed. "You serving dude?"

"Why not?"

"You know what it is between us. He my enemy, fam!"

"First of all, lower yo fuckin voice. I ain't one of them peons you be around. And second, what that gotta do wit me? You betta grow up. This shit bigger than Nino Brown. We do this for that cake and nothing or nobody else."

"You know what, you dead right." Gutta pulled his .380 from his waistband and smacked Arab across his face so hard his wrist bent back. Soon as Arab hit the floor, Gutta was on him.

He gripped the collar of his victim's shirt and repeatedly whacked on his face and head with the hard blue steel. "Fuck... You... Bitch." His words were venomous.

Arab lay on the floor bathing in his own blood as Gutta marched to the kitchen. Reaching in the top cabinet, he retrieved the spare Glock he knew would be there. Back in the living room, he stood over Arab, aiming the gun two inches from his right eye. "What you was saying now?"

"Chill, bruh, chill."

"Oh, you want me to chill, hunh? You straight bitch." Gutta made sure his hand was firm as he applied pressure to the trigger.

"Yo, Gutta!" Money, Dyco, and Q burst through the door, impeding him from finishing his deadly act. "Put that shit up, Gutta. Word." Dyco and Q had their guns aimed at Gutta. Money stood between Gutta and Arab.

"Watch out, Money. Dude gotta go."

"That shit dead. You know I can't let you do that."

"What? This disloyal nigga just served Torn."

"I know."

Money's response perplexed Gutta. "I know you ain't stamp that shit. Tell me you ain't stamp that shit, Money."

"I stamped it, bruh. This shit a business, Gutta. We can't let our emotions affect our pockets."

"Emotions? Business? Do you know what he did to Ebony, to my momma? How is that business?" Gutta was genuinely hurt. He felt like Money had crossed him. Defeated, he dropped the Glock to his side. "Damn." Tears welled in his eyes.

Money placed his hand on Gutta's shoulder and looked into his eyes. "That shit ain't bout nothing, word. I love you, my nigga, but at the end of the day, you gotta grow up. It's just not my business, Gutta. My business getting this bread."

Stunned with disbelief, he scooped his .380 from the floor and exited the apartment.

* * *

Mia strutted through the Williamsburg shopping outlet. Today was her 21st birthday and she was determined to find the perfect outfit to display her joy at finally being completely legal. Her entire week had been hectic with lawyer and jail visits in preparation for Gotti's preliminary hearing. After completing errands for everybody else, she swore that her weekend would be all about her.

Upon entering the BCBG clothing store, she removed her oversized sunshades. "Welcome to BCBG, may I assist you?" the Taylor Swift lookalike greeted her at the entrance with a jubilant expression.

"I just want to look around for now, thanks."

"Okay, I'll be right over here when you need me. My name's Karen."

"Okay, Karen."

Mia shopped the clothing racks, thinking of all the things she had planned for the day. Her closest friends had reserved the VIP section at Newport News' most notorious club named "The Alley." She couldn't wait for that to start so she could purchase her own liquor using her own ID for the first time. The after-party was scheduled to be at the Executive Hotel, where she had a suite for all of her closest associates. "You must not feel how I feel, oh I'm fresh," Mia sang the artist Future's song while holding an open-back black dress to her petite frame. For some reason she just couldn't get that song out of her head. "Excuse me, Karen."

The store's representative rushed to assist her. "Oh, you like that dress? That's from the latest fall collection We just put it on the shelf yesterday."

"Yeah, it's definitely fly."

"You can say that again." The girls laughed.

"I think I'mma get this."

"Perfect." Karen carefully carried the dress to the counter.

After choosing some matching heels, Mia was ready to complete her purchase. "Um…the total is one thousand, five hundred and thirty-five dollars. You might can just get it cheaper online."

Mia was thrown off by Karen's comment. "Nah, I'll get it here." Popping the latch on her Chanel clutch, she reached in, handing the lady 160 brand new one-hundred-dollar bills. "You said fifteen, right?" Usually she would've used her credit card, but she felt the urge to shine on the condescending worker. Karen grabbed the money awkwardly. "Keep the change, baby."

"Thanks. You come back anytime."

"I will." Mia strolled out the store with her head in the clouds.

Outside she popped the trunk on her brand new Barbie-pink Audi R8. Gotti had the car delivered to her that morning. Her smile was bright as a summer day as she recollected her elation when she saw the red ribbon attached to the hood. Gotti had really got her the best birthday gift ever.

Directly across the street the same elation could be seen, but for a completely different reason. Torn and Fatts sat in a black Denali, monitoring Mia's every move. "Look at this silly bitch trotting around like she bulletproof." Torn couldn't believe how lucky he was. He was meeting a customer in the outlet's parking lot when, out of nowhere, he noticed Mia driving by, looking like a guppy to the two piranhas.

"You want me to pop her or you gone pop her?" Fatts had his hand on his rubber-gripped pistol.

"Nah, this time somebody gone pay for my truck."

Fatts had a devilish grin. "Enough said."

Drifting through the parking lot, the Denali came to an abrupt halt behind Mia's Audi. Torn jumped out. Terror paralyzed her, making it effortless for him to drape a black sack over her face. Aggressively he tossed her in the trunk area of the SUV. Hopping in with her, he firmly applied layers of duct tape around her legs and arms. She found her voice and screamed until he placed duct tape over her mouth and covered her head back with the black sack. At this point she sobbed uncontrollably, wondering how the best birthday of her life could have possibly turned into her last.

* * *

I'mma real nigga/lick hitta/ bitch getta/quick flippa/pot whippa/dope deala/Fly nigga/pop off I'mma ride nigga/goyard a hundred racks inside nigga. Gutta stepped through the doors of the alley as Young Scooter's "Jugg King" blasted through the sound system. The building was packed to capacity. A majority of the club-goers were there to celebrate Mia's birthday. The rest just wanted to be a part of the festivities. Gutta was dressed impeccably, donning a tan Louis

Vuitton shirt with brown leather patches stitched on the shoulder, a custom-made Louis Vuitton belt with a gold-plated LV buckle, and denim Louis Vuitton jeans with brown leather LV logos stitched on the back pockets. The Louis Vuitton shoes he had custom made exquisitely completed the ensemble.

Lil Man, Tye, and M.A. rose when Gutta entered the VIP section. "What's up? Where you been at? We ain't even think you was gone show." Tye moved over so Gutta could sit.

"I been chilling, my nigga. I had to get my mind right."

"I heard bout that shit wit Money. If you trynna ride, just say the word."

"That shit ain't bout nothing, bruh."

Tye looked at Gutta skeptically. "Yeah, aight. I know you, bruh."

"I ain't even on that type time tonight, fam. I'm trynna get high, drunk, and chill."

Lil Man reached past Tye, handing Gutta a full bottle of Cîroc.

The night progressed beautifully. DJ Big Will was spinning a variety of the hottest music. Trap music, club music, reggae, dance hall, whatever your flavor, he was playing it. The mood was lit. M.A. convinced a gang of groupies to entertain the team with lap dances as they circulated multiple blunts of exotic weed.

Mia's cousin Nicole approached Gutta about an hour later, squeezing her body in the gap between him and Lil Man. "Yo, where Mia at?"

"I don't know, I thought she would've been with you."

"Nah, I been calling her since like five o'clock and she ain't answering."

"She might show up in a little bit."

"Nah, Gutta, forreal, I knew her all my life. She would've been here by now."

"Aight, what you want me to do?"

"I want you to give a fuck!"

"Yo, just relax. Let me go to the bathroom and call her. She might be ducking yo worrisome ass."

Gutta excused himself to the bathroom, navigating his way through the sea of overzealous patrons. The bathroom was a three-stall, two-sink broom closet with nearly seven people standing around holding up space. A group of males had lined up against the wall, waiting for their chance to occupy the facilities, when Gutta walked up. Disregarding the entire line, he walked straight through the doorway as two men stepped out. No one dared to contest or complain to the known murderer. They simply acted like they didn't notice the blatant disrespect. With his back against the far corner, he pulled his phone, scrolling to Mia's number before hitting send. *"You have reached the voice mail box of Mia, please leave…"* Gutta ended the call, hitting the redial button.

"Gutta… Gutta!" Mia briefly screamed into the receiver before the phone was snatched from her mouth.

"What's up, bitch," a male voice came across.

"Yo, where the fuck Mia at?"

"She a little tied up right now."

The audacity of the guy infuriated Gutta. "Who the fuck is this?"

"The angel of death here to send yo bitch ass home."

Gutta's heart raced at the revelation of who was on the other end. "Yo, everybody get the fuck out!" The bathroom's occupants scurried like roaches when the lights come on. Locking the door, Gutta resumed his call. "Yo, let me talk to Mia."

"Don't trip, homeboy, she alive...for now."

"That's some sucka shit, Torn. You kidnapping bitches now? I'm right here. Kidnap me, bitch."

Torn laughed hysterically. "Aww, that's cute, but look, this how shit bout to go down. You gone bring me a million dollars in the next thirty minutes or you gone find more pieces of this bitch than a Malaysia flight. I don't think big bruh Gotti gone be feeling that shit."

Gutta was furious. "What? You got me fucked up. You keep her. I'll just buy my brother another bitch." He ended the call.

Staring at his reflection, he didn't like the man staring back. Gotti would have never let Mia die, and he had just signed her death certificate. For a second he considered agreeing with the terms and paying the ransom. It was just something in him that wouldn't allow him to negotiate with terrorists. She would probably just end up dead anyway.

In a tantrum he threw a powerful jab at his reflection. "Fuck!" Blood trickled down his knuckles. The mirror now showed a shattered image of a defeated gangster. Wrapping his hands in paper towels, he exited the bathroom, vowing never to speak on the dreadful decision.

Back at the VIP, Gutta noticed Money had arrived with Q and Dyco. He reluctantly masked his displeasure. "What's good, bruh?" Money stood as Gutta ascended the VIP steps.

"Ain't shit. What's up?"

"Chillin. Came to show my love. Where the birthday girl at?"

"I don't know. Nicole was just looking for her."

"I need to holla at you before this night ova too."

"Bout what?"

"That's something for later."

Gutta took a seat on the lounge sectional. Three drinks later a girl he went to school with manifested from the crowd, attempting to gain entry to the VIP party area. "Excuse me, I'm wit the birthday party."

"I don't see yo name on the list." Rico, the head of security, was posted by the stairway like a Marine officer.

"Fuck that list. I know Gutta. I don't gotta be on no list."

"Heard that one before."

"Gutta! Gutta!"

Gutta searched for who was calling his name. He squinted in the dimly lit club, seeing Precious waving like she was trying to hail a taxi. Precious Jewel Polantino was one of the sexiest girls in his seventh grade class. For years he had a major crush on the black and Puerto Rican princess. Her butter-pecan complexion and 36-24-38 frame was something he had many sexual fantasies about as a youngster. Even though she was his class partner and school friend, he never had the gall to approach her for anything more than school work and conversation. He just always felt she was out of his league. As he watched her outside the VIP section with her all-red Freakum dress on, he couldn't help but thank God that today wasn't the seventh grade. "Yo, Rico, let her in."

Rico stood to the side, releasing the red velvet rope. "Thank you, damn." She pushed past the bouncer and strutted right up to Gutta. Bending down, she hugged his neck and kissed him on the cheek. "You need to learn how to tame yo dogs."

"He aight. What's up wit you, though? Have a seat with me." Money slid down so she could sit.

"Nothing. Just got back in town and heard the alley was going be jumping tonight, but I ain't expect it to be this turnt up."

"Yeah, today my brother wife birthday."

"Which one is she?" Precious looked around.

"She ain't here yet. Fuck that, though. I ain't seen you in a minute, shorty."

"I know. We moved to Atlanta right after my seventh grade year. I ain't really had no reason to come back to Va till now."

"Oh yeah? What's that?"

"I'm starting this job at Wells Fargo."

"That's aight, yo. You doing it, ain't you."

"Not yet. I'm trying, though. But I been hearing yo name since the second I crossed state lines. People talk about you like you the black John Gotti."

"You know how that go, shorty. Nowadays if they don't got a story, they'll make one."

"Yeah, right." Precious looked down to see the blood-soaked towels on his hand. "Oh my God! You bleeding."

Gutta had totally forgotten about his injuries. "That shit ain't nothing. I got it caught in the bathroom door." Money, overhearing this explanation, eyed Gutta suspiciously.

Precious held his hand out and poured a bottle of Dasani water that sat on the table over his wounds. Going in her red Coach purse, she retrieved a pack of Kleenex and dried his hand.

"That ain't enough. If you gone take care of a nigga, you gotta kiss it and make it feel better."

Precious blushed before pressing her lips to his knuckles. "Better?"

"Much better."

"Boy, you still silly as hell. Trynna be all Casanova. I remember when you had them dingy ass all-white Air Forces."

"What! How you got jokes when you wore the same Juicy t-shirt you got from Rainbows every week."

"Nigga, fuck you." The tandem laughed.

"For real, though, Precious, I'm glad you here, shorty. You don't know how much I needed to laugh."

"Well, I'm glad I could do that for you." The couple blocked the noise and enjoyed each other's company while the party ensued around them.

After about three more hours, the people who were there for Mia retired the hopes of her gracing them with her presence and conducted themselves like it was just any other club night. Around 2:30 in the morning, when the club only had about 30 minutes left, the crowd began to diminish. Money rose to exit as well. "Yo, Gutta, walk wit me outside."

Gutta took one last shot of Cîroc and said goodbye to Precious. The pair strolled through the parking lot in relative silence. Money's CLS 550 Benz was stationed near the back exit of the club. Pressing the button on his key chain, his trunk elevated. Gutta stepped back, attempting to see what was in the trunk. "Pull up, bruh." He cautiously approached, viewing two large, black travel suitcases.

"What's this?"

"This the next level." Money unzipped the cargo. Inside the first bag was bales of cash, spilling over the side after being decompressed. The second contained over 100 kilos of raw cocaine. Gutta was flabbergasted. "This our future. It's no limit to where I'm bout to take us in this game," Money said.

Gutta took a step back. "This yo future. I'm bout to do my own thing from now on."

"Do yo own thing? Fuck that's supposed to mean?"

"You once taught me if a nigga show you a flaw, then that flaw really exist. You told me that. So how you expect me to trust you and be all fraudulent after what you showed me the other day?"

Money slammed the trunk shut. "You still bitching bout that shit? Pull yo fucking skirt down, fam. Real shit."

Money's brazenness incensed Gutta. Stepping back, he reached in the small of his back, brandishing his compact .40 caliber Millennium Taurus.

Money never looked at the gun, only at Gutta, using his eyes as the windows to his soul. "You know what you just did, Gutta?"

"I know exactly what I'm doing. You ain't for me, fam. It's Newport Nam out this bitch and you funding the opposition. Giving my enemy money to compete wit me, buy bullets to riddle me wit, and I'm posed to still fuck wit you. Nah, not Gutta. I'm not that nigga."

Gutta's eyes betrayed his intentions. Money could tell when someone had the thirst for blood. Right now he knew that thirst was prevalent in Gutta. His eyes were the eyes that haunted his nightmares since he was a teenager. For years he dreamed of the man who would take his life. He just didn't recognize the face until this very second. Karma had finally come to cash in her raincheck. "So this what it come to, after all I done for you and bruh. I gave you niggas hope when you had nothing. How now can you doubt me? I let you in my family when you had nobody. Now you wanna try to out me. You can't kill me, Gutta. You fucking need me."

"I need you? You can't be serious. I got ten reasons to pull this trigger, and right now you ain't giving me one reason not to."

"How bout me being the only one that can free yo brother? That good enough?"

"Free my brother? How the fuck can you free Gotti? You ain't got no get-out-of-jail-free card."

"I'm the one that put him there. All I gotta do is recant and we go our separate ways."

Gutta was speechless. With his gun aimed at Money's chest, he recollected the many disappearances and suspect comments that never sat right with him. He reflected on Torn's devious grin, Ebony's bloody body, and Mia's last words. It was beginning to be too much for him. The revelation of Money's disloyalty added fuel to his already volatile thinking process. "I'm got it, my nigga. I'mma free him right now." Gutta emptied the magazine in his chest, putting more holes in him than a fisher's net.

Money's eyes remained open, staring at the heavens. It appeared he was praying that the gates opened for him. Sadly, as his life drained from his body, it was evident the devil already had a spot reserved right next to him in hell.

Chapter 14

I'm in this for the long haul/If death should us part through thick and thin I won't pretend/I'm in this for the long haul/Loyalty is something naturally instilled/miles away hard to smile some days. Gotti posted with his back against the wall by his cell, listening to the sincere words of rappers Kevin Gates and Starlito. He hadn't spoken to his brother in weeks. Daily he replayed their last conversation in his mind. Gutta's words stung like salt to his wounds. A long time ago he vowed to always be his brother's keeper. Unfortunately his incarceration had hindered that promise dramatically. The streets seemed to be claiming his brother and there was nothing he could do about it.

"Nephew, nephew."

Gotti removed his earbuds. "What's up, D.P.?"

"I see you ain't been at that poker table lately. How you feeling?"

"I'm good, just got a lot on my mental, that's all."

D.P. placed his back to the wall also. "This shit ain't getting rough for you, is it?"

"Hold up right quick." Gotti wrapped his earbuds up and stuck them in his pocket. He was always attentive when D.P. spoke. The 40-year-old Pan-Africanist was honestly one of the wisest dudes he met in his life. His views and insights on politics, the African culture, and life in general was a form of education the school system would never allow. His genuine respect for the man allowed him to always accept whatever jewels he was willing to deliver. "My bad.

Yeah, though I just been having my brother on my mind tough lately. I told you bout that situation already, right?"

"Yeah, you did, but you can't let that get you down, lil bruh. You just gotta love him for who he is, not who you want or expected him to be."

"I feel you, but Gutta my heart. We been through everything together. Rose from the dirt forreal. Now he trynna carry me like I ain't shit. Don't even answer my calls no more. Something changing in my nigga, D.P. I know it, I can feel it."

"Youngblood, that's how it is when you make a man. That's why a man gotta learn to make himself. Then you shake his hand."

Gotti absorbed the quote. As he adapted it to memory, he noticed the pod had congregated in front of the TV for the local WAVY News 10 broadcast.

"Gotti, they talkin bout round the way." He walked up but stood at the back of the crowd. He wanted a little better view but still made sure he was out the way.

Breaking news flashed across the screen. "A deadly shooting leaves one dead in a nightclub parking lot. Taurus Austin was found slain with ten bullet wounds to his chest behind The Alley nightclub in Newmarket shopping center. A security guard discovered his riddled corpse after closing hours. There are no leads at this time but detectives are thoroughly investigating this homicide."

Gotti recognized Money's government name immediately. Somebody had murdered his friend in cold blood. When he thought it couldn't any worse, it did. His nightmare materialized in the form of a news anchor's words. "Another developing story comes out of Williamsburg, Virginia. Somewhere around four o'clock this morning, the corpse of a Newport News native was discovered in a burning Camry in the Busch Gardens parking lot. Jamia Brown was found brutally tortured and shot to death on her twenty-first birthday. Firefighters responding rapidly to the call of a burning vehicle were fortunately able to extinguish the flames before any major damage was done to her body. No leads or motives are available at this time. If you have any information that could assist in solving either one of these heinous crimes, please contact Newport News police at 1-888-LOCK-U-UP."

The reporter dealt a crushing blow to Gotti's spirit. His tears were unrestrainable and his pain was unbearable. He stared blankly at the TV screen. The usually rowdy pod had quieted. Overcome with misery, he sluggishly walked to his cell to grieve in private.

* * *

Money's funeral was held at Miracle Temple Baptist Church. The entire Tidewater area attended to show support. Hustlers and gangsters alike traveled from all over Virginia, packing every row and lining the walls when no seats were available. The feds even had a van stationed outside, flashing pictures of the industry's elite.

Gucci sat in the front row with Money's grieving family. The past week had been hell for her. Her nights were restless and her days were filled with hallucinations of her deceased lover. The dismal atmosphere of the church was hard for her to bear. After days of crying, her tear ducts had dried up like a desert well, and her stoic expression was used to conceal her grief.

Bishop Ken Froberg presided over the service. Bishop Ken was an older Caucasian male who made it his life's mission to spread the gospel to inner city youths. Working as a house arrest officer for the city provided him with the ideal situation to reach as many lives as possible.

Money had been one of his prospects as a juvenile. Even though he chose to travel a different path in life, Mr. Froberg still prayed for him and Money always appreciated his blessings.

Gutta arrived just as the eulogy was scheduled to be given. He hated attending funerals. The screams of grieving widows and family members always made him reflect on the countless lives he dismantled. Some insignificant female who probably had never even spoken to Money slid over as Gutta entered the church. He removed his Gucci shades out of respect for the religious temple.

"We are here to celebrate the life of Taurus Austin." The bishop paced the stage, gripping a microphone. "Some of you knew him personally. Some of you did not. For those who did, some will say he was a good, honest man, a true angel of God and a blessing to those he embraced. On the other hand, some of you would indeed argue the contrary. Whatever your views, we all must agree to one fact: that he was at least worthy of our opinions. His spirit deeply affected those he encountered, including mine. Not too long ago I ran into him at a local Wendy's. His smile glowed like the Lord's halo as he walked to me, smothering me with those strong arms of his. We sat and talked for hours that day. During that conversation I told him that I honestly had never stopped praying for him. Unexpectedly he ask me one simple question: Why? I tell you all today what I told him then. I said, Taurus, you're just too real to be forgotten." The congregation erupted in a thunderous applause.

Gutta sat in the back, shaking his head at the naïve participants. To him Money was no more than a snake in wolf's clothing. The scene sickened him. Once upon a time Money had been a mentor and friend. Today animosity accompanied every thought of him.

Pop! Gutta felt a sharp pain to his temple. Arab had ambushed him from the side in the middle of the church. Jumping back after his assault, Arab bounced with his hands up, ready to box with God. Gutta went ballistic, charging at his cowardly attacker. A group of Samaritans quickly formed a blockade between the two enemies, impeding his retaliation. "Get the fuck out my way." The civilians didn't budge.

"What is y'all doing?!" Gucci barked with her hands balled into fists.

"This nigga killed Money!" Arab roared. Gutta had a dumbfounded look on his face.

"What he talking bout, Gutta?" Gucci was looking at Gutta with tears in her eyes.

"Fuck what he talking bout. That bitch ass nigga just snuck me. I gotta have him."

Gucci pushed Gutta back and stepped directly in his face. Her eyes were bloodshot red as tears streamed down her cheeks. "What he talking bout, Gutta?!"

Her solemn expression sent chills through his body. "What you mean? How I'm posed to know?"

"Look me in my eyes and tell me you ain't kill him…tell me you ain't kill my husband, please."

Gutta stared directly in her eyes. "Sis, I love you, and no, I didn't kill him." His gaze was unwavering.

She stared at him for five seconds before pivoting towards Arab. "Get the fuck outta here."

"What? He lying, Gucci! Ms. Austin, he lying! I know he did it!"

"Can somebody get him outta here?"

The men of the congregation began forcibly escorting Arab from the building. Enraged at being ejected, he shouted obscenities the whole way out.

Chapter 15

"Walker, attorney visit." The air pressure was released on his cell's automatic door. Gotti exited, pulling his green jail-issued uniform top over his head. It was a week until his preliminary hearing, and this was the first time his lawyer had been to see him. Numerous times he thought of firing the greedy mafioso but was constantly talked out of it by his dearly departed Mia. Callahan had been the family's go-to attorney for any legal proceedings. For the right price, he would wheel and deal with all walks of life to guarantee a favorable outcome.

CO Williams, a voluptuous-bodied female from Portsmouth, was tasked with the duty of escorting Gotti. "What's up, Ms. Williams."

"Hey, Walker, you feeling better?"

"Yeah, I'm good. Tough times don't last, tough niggas do."

"I hear that."

The pair rode the elevator to the second floor where the visitation area was located. "You in the second booth." Ms. Williams led Gotti to his designated cubicle and locked him in the transparent room.

Mr. Callahan arrived ten minutes later, sweating like he just finished running the Boston Marathon. "Mr. Walker, how you feeling today?"

"I'm feeling like I need another lawyer. Why you just now coming a day before my preliminary?"

"My apologies, I was out of town on vacation. I told Ms. Brown during our last visit to inform you of this."

"She probably would have if she wasn't dead."

Callahan was shocked. "Dead?"

"Yeah, dead, but you would've known that if she owed you some money."

"I'm sorry to hear that, Mr. Walker. My deepest condolences."

"Man, fuck that. What up with this case?"

"Well, I talked to the prosecutor, a Mr. David Schultz, yesterday. It seems they have a confidential informant who agrees to provide specific details relating to the murder of Marcus Knight."

"Who is he?"

"That's probably gonna be kept under wraps until he's called to testify."

"So what up wit a bond?"

"Hold your horses for a second. The state's offering a chance to avoid a lengthy trial. Just tell them anything you know about the case and you plead to simple involuntary manslaughter. One to ten tops."

Gotti scowled at the indolent attorney. "I want you to listen to me closely. Never, I mean never will I testify, cop out for a plea, or surrender information on my boys to police. So don't ever insult my character like that again."

Callahan turned red as a menstrual cycle. "Understood. I guess I'll see you in court tomorrow."

"I guess so." Gotti rose and beat on the glass while Callahan rushed to gather his belongings.

Ms. Williams unlocked the door for him to exit. "Wow, if looks could kill, gosh almighty."

"My bad, shorty. I just hate when people try to play me."

"I guess it wasn't good news, hunh?"

"It for real ain't no news. Cracker think I'm going out like Nicki Barnes or somebody."

"You don't know how many people I bring to these meetings and find out later they done piggybacked on somebody case, so I wouldn't be surprised."

"I ain't that nigga, shorty. I come from the dirt. It's just in my DNA to hold water."

"Well, I'm glad it's still some real niggas out there." Ms. Williams walked Gotti back to three-one pod and went on break. Gotti's pedigree stayed on her mind for hours. She wouldn't admit it but inwardly she was infatuated with the suspected murderer.

* * *

The next day Gotti was transported to Newport News city jail for his preliminary hearing. He hadn't slept the entire night. He was just too anxious to learn his fate. As he paced the small holding cell outside of Judge Pugh's courtroom, he mulled over his decision to let Callahan continue his representation. He strongly considered relieving the man of his duties, but decided as much as Mia went through convincing him to have faith in the attorney, he would at least see how it turned out initially.

The locks on the room turned. "Walker, your attorney's here," Deputy Kelly announced.

Gotti was ushered to a non-contact booth. Callahan sat on the opposite side of a thick glass divider, studying his files. "Mr. Walker, how you hanging in there?"

"Long as they don't hang me out there, I'm good."

Callahan smiled. "Well, I just finished conferring with the prosecutor, and it seems they have an issue with the evidence."

"What type of issue?"

"The confidential informant is no longer available to testify."

Gotti's euphoria was evident. "So what they gone do?"

"It's still up to his discretion. He can either proceed with whatever else he does have, which to my knowledge is little to none, or he can non-process your charge. If he does continue, it's a good chance the judge will dismiss it anyway. Now nothing's a sure bet, but if I were you, I would start making plans for my release."

"Damn right!" Gotti shot up from his seat, shaking his fist in the air.

"Just remain calm, Mr. Walker, and by the end of the day, you should be a free man."

"Good looks." Gotti was placed in the holding tank. Even though he was elated with the news, he couldn't deny the bittersweet feeling. He dreamed many nights of Mia's beautiful smile and tender kisses greeting him at the gate. Her death had been the one defining moment in his incarceration. The pain he felt mourning the loss of his love was entirely too much for him to digest. Callahan told him to plan for his release. Unbeknownst to him, Gotti's plan had been devised the moment he saw Mia's face on the news.

Twenty minutes later he was led into the courtroom. As he stood behind the mahogany defense table, he was floored to see his mother sitting in the second row. Dressed in a flowing sundress with open-toe sandals, her angelic smile radiated throughout the room. Ms. Tina had finally beat her addiction. After years of seeing his mother's decrepit frame, her immaculate and healthy appearance nearly brought tears to his eyes. Beside her was Gucci, waving like she was on a float in the Southeast Day parade.

"All rise," the bailiff announced as Judge Pugh entered.

"Be seated." Judge Pugh placed his telescope-style reading glasses over his eyes. Banging his gavel twice, he brought the court into order. "Okay, I see here we have the State versus Jaxavier Walker in nineteen-point-two-dash-eight-two, the first degree murder of Marcus Knight, case number zero-one-two-nine-six-two, is that correct?"

"Yes, Your Honor, that's correct," David Schultz, a chubby white nationalist, answered from behind the prosecutor's table.

"Mr. Walker, do you fully understand these charges and know that if convicted, could carry a maximum sentence of life imprisonment without possibility of parole?"

Callahan nodded for Gotti to answer. "Yes, sir."

"With that in mind, how do you plead?"

"Not guilty."

Pugh scribbled in his notes. "Let the record show that the defendant pleads not guilty to the charges against him. Mr. Schultz, are you ready to proceed?"

"Your Honor, at this time I would like to request a continuance." Gotti nearly had a brain aneurysm.

"On what grounds?" the judge asked.

"Well, we recently lost our star witness to a senseless homicide last week and would like time to regroup and prepare a more compelling case."

Judge Pugh looked to the defense table. "Callahan."

"Your Honor, I object to the continuance. My client has been patiently incarcerated for months now. It is my understanding that this deceased witness is the only evidence connecting my client to any part of this case. In turn I would like to respectfully move for a dismissal due to a sheer lack of evidence."

David Schultz was livid. "Your Honor, this is a dangerous man. He has been the suspect in numerous homicides and is currently being federally investigated for drug trafficking. It will be a horrendous error to release this animal into society."

Judge Pugh dropped his pen, removed his glasses, and rubbed the bridge of his nose. "Mr. Schultz, I too believe that animals should be removed from our society and thrown into cages where they belong. Fortunately I also believe that we are a country of laws. As an officer of the court, I am sworn to uphold that law regardless of my personal beliefs. I cannot keep a man incarcerated based on your assumptions, and you have presented no evidence worthy of a continuance. Mr. Walker, at this time it is my ruling that your case be dismissed and you be released. Thank you, gentleman."

"Judge, you're making a huge mistake! I beg you to reconsider!" David Schultz was red as Snow White's apple.

"I said thank you, gentleman!" The judge banged his gavel.

Ms. Tina and Gucci shrieked with excitement. Gotti rose, shook Callahan's hand, and was transported back to the regional to be processed out.

Later that night at the Bonefish Grill restaurant, a newly freed Gotti was enjoying a delicious dinner with Gucci and his mother. The emotional reunion earlier that day would forever be embedded in the minds of all involved. For Gotti it symbolized him getting his life back. The modern-day slavery of incarceration was an experience he vowed never to repeat. Gucci was just excited to be gaining a loved one after losing so much the past couple weeks. For her it was a major step in her healing process. Ms. Tina was more happy for herself than Gotti. The expression on his face when he hugged his mother spoke volumes of how proud he was of her. His approval was all she desired.

"Damn, Ma, you look good," Gotti constantly commended his mother's recovery.

"I do, don't I, love." She struck a pose.

"Girl, bye." Gucci pursed her lips, waving Ms. Tina off.

"Oh, don't hate, Gucci."

"Hate? Anyway, Gotti, I know you happy to be out."

"Yeah. I can't front, though, it don't feel the same."

"Mia, right?"

"Yeah. I just always expected her to be here. She ain't deserve that, sis. Word, she didn't."

"I know, Gotti. Sometimes we gotta lean on the serenity prayer for guidance and just accept things, knowing that it's all in God's plan."

"Yeah, that shit don't make it feel no better, though."

"You might not be trynna hear this right now, but sooner or later you gone get it, forreal. I'm thinking bout giving my life over to Christ."

Gotti chuckled. "Come on, Gucci, miss me with—"

"Just listen!" Gucci's voice elevated. "We can't keep doing this, Gotti. Haven't we lost enough? If anybody should understand, it should be you. I'm tired, bruh. We can't follow the same roads and expect different outcomes. We'll never win this way. What we gotta lose by putting our faith in Jesus? I don't know bout you but I don't see nothing worth holding on to except our family." Tears created trails down her cheeks.

The truthfulness in her words created goosebumps on Gotti's arms. "I hear you, sis, forreal. I don't know if I'm ready but I definitely hear you."

"Let's just pray." The family bowed their heads. "God, grant us the serenity to accept the things we cannot change, the courage to change the things we can, and the wisdom to know the difference."

Her words reverberated through Gotti's conscience. He wanted desperately to travel the path less traveled. Sadly, he was already set in a different direction. The one leading him straight to vengeance.

Chapter 16

"Rise and shine, boi." Gutta groggily stirred to find Damian, Chanta, and a room full of Jamaicans hovering over his bed. The various assault rifles pointed at him incinerated all hopes of this being a friendly visit.

"What's up, fam? What's all this?"

"Ya know, boi. I tell me breadren when I see ya de first time ya pride would kill ya one day." Precious, who was asleep beside him, abruptly woke up, screaming to the top of her lungs. The sight of the Jamaicans with guns was equivalent to the grim reaper with his axe to her. "Silence, gal, fa I haffi murda ya."

"Precious, shut the fuck up, shorty." Gutta knew Damian would have no problem silencing her if she didn't. "Look, Dame, I don't know what all this bout, but I definitely don't appreciate the disrespect."

Chanta stepped up, pressing the barrel of a baby AK to Gutta's skull. "Shut ya bumla mouth, boi."

Damian put his hand on the small of Chanta's back. "Relax. Gutta, ya murda da wrong person dis time, breadren. Ya don't know fuckin wit my currency like fuckin wit my mutha."

Damian's words unveiled his quarrel. "Look, Damian, Money had to go. He threatened my safety. That shit was business, nothing personal wit you at all."

"Forty-eight hours. Ya got forty-eight hours to get my tree million dollars or I prove ta ya I da original Dundada." The Jamaicans exited, leaving Gutta to collect his thoughts.

His nerves were taxed as he threw his head back on the feather-stuffed pillows. Beside him Precious lay, still sniffling. "Yo, get dressed and get the fuck out." She hurriedly snatched her clothes off the floor and ran.

Lying there, he analyzed his predicament. He had just spent the majority of his money funding the clothing factory. Producing another $3 million would surely be a strenuous task. *Ding.* The sound alerted him to a new Facebook message. Grabbing his iPhone 6 from the nightstand, he checked his page. The image he saw lifted the weight from his shoulders like a champion body builder. Gotti had his arms stretched and his head bowed like Jesus when he was crucified. Under it the caption read simply: *Touchdown to Cause Hell.* Lying back, he placed his hands under his head and stared at the ceiling. Ironically, the post was perfect cause right now he desperately needed a savior.

* * *

I gotta hold on/cause I been struggling for so long/seems like when I try to right/it goes wrong. Gotti and Lump pulled up to the Aberdeen graveyard with Lil Boosie's "Here We Go Again" blaring from the trunk. After getting himself together, Lump had picked him up in his 2011 Porsche Cayman. There was a list of items on Gotti's to-do list but none more important than visiting the grave of his lost love. "Hold up, bruh, I'mma be like five seconds."

"Take yo time, my nigga."

Gotti leisurely made his way through the graveyard. It was hard for him to compose his emotions, knowing how close he was to Mia's beautiful corpse. Tears crept from his eye wells as he stood in front of the headstone reading: *Here rests God's greatest creation, Jamia Brown.* He kneeled, placing the bouquet of roses at the headstone's base. "Damn, bae, never in a million years could I have prepared to be standing here right now. I fucked up, bae. I should've been there. I promised to always protect you, and all I end up doing was getting you killed. I'll carry that pain with me for the rest my life, bae. I will forever love you, Mia. Today, tomorrow, always." He kissed his fingers and touched her name before heading back to the car.

As he entered, Lump was smoking a blunt. "You good?" he asked.

"Yeah, I'm good. Let's get outta here." Reaching over, he hit the button on Lump's sound system, changing to a more suitable Boosie song: "Retaliation, It's Payback."

* * *

"A week of murders have left four dead and three in critical condition in the uptown area of Newport News. The city's chief of police has requested the public's assistance in their attempts at bringing peace and safety to the citizens of this great city. There is a one-thousand-dollar reward for any information leading to the arrest of any of the week's culprits. Please call 1-888-LOCK-U-UP. That's 1-888-LOCK-U-UP."

Torn and Fatts lounged in Fatts' Aqueduct apartment, watching the Channel 10 news broadcast. "What the fuck!" Torn banged his hand against the chair's armrest. He was furious. The week since Gotti's release, his team had been assassinated like American soldiers on Al-Queda soil. The slaying of his closest friends and partners was beginning to be too much for him to handle.

"Chill, my nigga, everything straight," Fatts said.

His nonchalant demeanor was really irritating Torn. "Everything straight? Our niggas dying out there and you eating chips, talking bout everything straight."

"I'm just saying shit be like that sometime."

"They killed Tone, my nigga, Tone. Shit not posed to be like that, fam."

"Word."

Torn looked at Fatts and shook his head. "This nigga crazy." His phone vibrated on the kitchen counter. "Yo," he answered without bothering to check the Caller ID. Whoever it was immediately captured his attention. A devilish smile spread on his face. Ending the call, he grabbed his keys from atop the refrigerator. "Fatts, come on, my nigga. We out."

* * *

"Why you always on the phone?"

"My bad."

Gucci and Ebony relaxed in the vibrating chairs at K Nails in Newmarket shopping center. A couple days earlier Gucci sent Ebony a Facebook message, insisting she attend church with her. She even Facebook-Lived her request, forcing Ebony to consent. After Money's funeral Gucci had completely changed her lifestyle, becoming a devout Christian. She made it her mission to do the Lord's work, saving as many souls as possible. Today the service was beautiful. At one point both ladies had got overwhelmed with the Holy Spirit. Gucci even shouted in a bizarre language and fainted. By the end of the program, Ebony was quoting the pastor's words, giving her life over to Christ.

"Who was that anyway?" Gucci asked.

"Nobody important."

"Oh, how you like church today?"

"Girl, it was wonderful. I did not expect none of that. I really got moved and everything."

"I know. Our God is a wonderful God, ain't he?"

"Yes, he is."

"I hear that, praise Jesus." The girls high-fived.

Moments later Ebony hung her head, captivated in her thoughts. "What's up, girl? Talk to me?" Gucci asked Ebony, noticing her spirits were troubled.

"Well, I'm kinda scared, sis."

"Scared of what?"

"I mean, I know God blessed me with another life, but what if I ain't worth it? What if I end up doing something I just can't be forgiven for?"

Gucci placed her fingers under Ebony's chin, lifting her head. "Listen to me. When I say God is good, it's not cause it sound good. Our entire life is designed by him. In the end his will be done, so whatever you have done or will do, he knows. Trust me, you are already forgiven. He just want you to ask for it."

Ebony's heart melted. "You are truly beautiful, Gucci. Inside and out."

"That's only cause I'm made in his image."

"You done," the Chinese nail technician announced.

"She crushed them jaints, girl." The pair examined Gucci's toenail design.

"Yes, she did."

After paying and tipping the lady, they left the shop, cautiously stepping across the parking lot, careful not to smear the polish. It took all of five minutes to reach Gucci's red Infiniti Audi R8. "Girl, I don't know how I'mma open this door without messing my nails up."

"Stop being so prissy all the time. Matter of fact, I got you." Ebony opened Gucci's driver side door before walking to the passenger. "Oh my God." Ebony froze as she stared past Gucci at the black Denali. Tears began gushing from her eyes.

"What, girl? What's wrong?" Gucci was concerned with Ebony's terrified expression. Ebony's mouth moved but no words came out. Gucci studied her lips, trying to decipher what she was saying. "You sorry. You sorry for what?"

Suddenly she felt her head jerk back. Fatts pressed the rag drenched in chloroform over her mouth and nose. Ebony threw her arms on the car's roof and dropped her head in her arms, flooded with regret. Gucci flailed, scratched, and kicked her legs until she was no longer able to resist. Succumbing to the powerful chemical, she fainted right into her kidnapper's arms.

* * *

Gucci saw two of everything as she woke groggily. The effects of the chloroform had her head pounding like a Hampton University drummer. The thick coiled rope tied around her arms and legs restricted her to a cold steel chair. A red bandana covered her mouth, muffling any potential screams. The continuous drip from a rusty pipe was the only sound she could hear. Surveying the room, she could tell it was some sort of basement. The room was dimly lit and reeked of decaying mold. Beads of sweat formed over her brow. She tried desperately to suppress the terror she was feeling. Her futile efforts at freeing her arms from the restraints aggravated her.

"She's alive! She's alive!" Torn, Fatts, and Bud descended the wooden steps. "How you doing, beautiful?" Bud removed the bandana from her mouth, wiping her eyes and nose with his sleeve. "You gone be aight, cheer up."

"Please let me go. I ain't do nothing."

"I wish it was that simple, gorgeous." Torn leaned against the wall, staring at his captive. "What you think, Fatts?"

"Let's just kill her and be done wit it."

"I was thinking that too."

"Hold on one second. What type shit y'all on? We ain't at least gone get no bread?" Torn and Fatts looked at each other and burst into laughter. "Damn, I wanna laugh too?"

"My nigga, we tried that wit the Mia bitch. That nigga Gutta tight as flea pussy."

"Bro, that was a bitch. This they sister. Plus Gotti home. He just not gone let her die. I know that for a fact."

Torn studied his options. "You might got a point."

"Man, let me find out Bud got soft. The nigga almost did bone marrow surgery on yo ass and you trynna compromise. Unbelievable," Fatts said, upset with the direction things were going in.

"Fuck you, Fatts. I ain't say not kill her. I said let's get this bread first. Tell me where that don't make sense."

"Whatever, dawg. Torn, what up? What you trynna do? I vote we kill her, he trynna save the hoe, so it's on you."

"I gotta betta idea. I say we kill two birds with one stone. Today must be yo lucky day, Ms. Gucci, cause you gone be that stone."

Chapter 17

Gotti arrived at Dunns River Jamaican restaurant in his quarter-million-dollar Ferrari F430. Jay-Z's "You Must Love Me" knocked from his speakers. His mother, Ms. Tina, called that morning, demanding he meet her for lunch. She was already seated when he entered smoking a Newport cigarette. "What's up, Ma?" He bent, kissing her on the cheek.

"Boy, don't kiss me smelling like a Bingo hall."

"Aight, Ma. You always doing the most."

"Boy, sit down."

Gotti unzipped his black Kush Kloud hoodie, draping it on the back of his seat. "So what you order?"

"I didn't yet, I was waiting on you." Glancing over Gotti's shoulder, she displayed her most charming face. "Son, do you love me?"

"What type of question is that? I ain't got no choice but to love you."

"Good, cause I need you not to leave."

"Leave for what?" Gotti traced Ms. Tina's eyes to the door where Gutta was entering. "Man, you bugging, Ma."

"Just chill, Gotti, dang."

Gutta approached the table and pointed at Gotti. "What, he bout to leave or something?"

"Nigga, you betta put that finger down fore I sever that shit."

"Ain't nobody going nowhere or severing nothing. I need to speak to both of y'all together." Ms. Tina's voice demanded respect.

Gotti rose, snatching his hoodie. "This shit dead."

"I got cancer, Gotti." Ms. Tina's blurt caused silence to eclipse the restaurant.

"What?"

"I need y'all to sit down." This time she sounded defeated. The brothers relented, grabbing seats at the table. "I was diagnosed last week with stage four cancer. The doctors say I gotta start aggressive chemo if I'mma have a chance." Her words paralyzed her sons. "Well, say something."

"What we posed to say, Ma? It's always something. Win one battle to fight another one. It's crazy. We actually live just to suffer." Gutta was choking on his words.

"That's what I wanted to speak wit y'all about. This battle…" She pointed to both brothers. "This battle one that don't gotta get fought cause ain't no winners at the end of the day. I can't say I raised y'all no type of way but I never expected y'all to act like this towards each other. Y'all brothers." Both men were void of responses. "Y'all ain't gotta say nothing, but before I leave this earth, I'mma make sure my family straight."

Gotti reached in his pocket for his phone that was now vibrating. *Unknown* flashed on the screen. "Yo, who dis?"

"You already know."

Gotti quickly recognized the voice. "Why you on my line, fam? Unless you committing suicide, we ain't got nothing to talk about."

"Suicide, please. What, you mad I got yo wifey on my belt?"

Gotti pressed the end button, disconnecting the call. Immediately his phone buzzed, alerting him to a new text message. His heart dropped as he opened his messenger. A disturbing picture of Gucci tied to a chair displayed on the screen. She had a bandana in her mouth and a nine SIG Sauer pointed to her temple. "What the fuck."

"What, Gotti, what is it?" Ms. Tina snatched the phone from Gotti's hand. Her gasp was heart-wrenching. The phone dropped from her hand, crashing to the floor.

"Yo, y'all trippin." Gutta anxiously fished the device, only to see an all too familiar vision. Plenty of nights he visioned Mia sitting in the exact same position, begging for her life.

Moments later the phone vibrated again. Gotti didn't hesitate to answer. "Let my sister go, fam, word."

"Why niggas act like cause they say word, that shit posed to mean something? You ain't got no juice, Gotti, none."

"Aight, you got it. I'm done. Just let my sister go and we can squash it."

"Don't insult me, muthafucka. This been beyond that point. Let's see if you stupid as yo brother. I need two million or the next time you see this bitch, she gone be butt naked, hanging from the James River Bridge. Now try me." Torn oozed venom.

"I promise you, Torn, you hurt my sister and you gone wish you was in that box with yo brother."

"You got till nine o'clock, my nigga, nine, cause at nine-o-one I'm lynching this po ass bitch." The phone went dead.

Ms. Tina instantly became distraught. Her cries echoed throughout the restaurant. "Calm down, Ma. It's gone be aight." Gotti wrapped his arms around her.

"You gotta get her back, Gotti. Get my baby back!"

"I am. How much bread you got, Gutta?"

"To be real, I only got bout a mil left."

"Damn. What, you took a loss or something?"

"Man, I got otha shit going on. You ain't gotta count my dollars."

"Fuck it, I got the rest."

"Gotti, you can't be that green. You think they really gone let her go? We pay 'em, they still gone kill her."

"So what, you suggesting we try 'em and hope they don't hang our sister? Really, that's yo plan?"

"Pretty much. We gotta call they bluff."

Gotti was disgusted with his brother. "Yo, you sick, bruh, word."

"Stop it!" Ms. Tina roared. "Y'all bickering like teenage bitches while my daughter tied up like some rodeo goat."

"Ma, let's be real. Ain't no need to give these dudes two million dollars when we all know they gone kill her anyway. Look what they did to Mia. They not gone let her go."

Gotti pondered these words. As much as he wanted it not to be true, deep down he knew what Gutta said made perfect sense. He had killed Torn's brother. There was no scenario where he would just let Gucci go, no matter how much he paid. "Gutta, you right. Let's go."

"Where we going?"

"To get our sister back."

* * *

Please, Please just leave me alone/I ain't bout no trouble but I could be/I'm just trynna get this cash again/but they make me turn into the bad guy again. Boosie blared through the surround sound system at Gotti's massive estate. He had his entire team assembled to formulate a strategy that would bring Gucci home and end the war. Hours earlier Torn reestablished contact, laying out his demands on how the money should be delivered. He wanted Gotti and Gutta alone to walk the cash to the back of Aqueduct apartments and wait. Gotti relayed the plans to his soldiers. "Man, fuck naw. For all that y'all might as well wear C-4 strapped to y'all chest," M.A. adamantly objected. Not one person liked the plan.

Gotti was to the point he was actually liking M.A.'s suggestion after losing his love, his homeboys, and now his sister's death didn't seem that far from heaven. "They can't be serious," Lil Man said.

"Fuck it. If y'all going, I'm going too. Give me some of that C-4," Lump added.

The brothers were surrounded by the core members of their squad. Lil Man, Lump, M.A., K.T., and Hot Boy all showed up, ready to ride in the name of loyalty. Gotti made sure he mended the fences with Lump and Gutta. With the promise of ten free bricks, the Kush Kloud clique was anxious to put the drama behind and work towards the future. Gutta even went a step further, offering a semi-apology to the 21st team. He attributed his mindset to his stressful situation, compounded by the loss of his brother. Lump, being just as close to his siblings, fully understood and gratefully accepted.

Gotti retrieved his war chest from his underground safe. Popping the lid, he presented the team with more weapons than Dr. Dre did on the movie *Set It Off*. The army green box was stocked with everything from Glock 9s to grenade launchers. Each soldier chose his weapon of choice and were given bulletproof vests capable of stopping cop-killing shells on impact. The plan was simple: Get Gucci, kill Torn. All they had to do now was execute, which would be like climbing a wall with cinderblocks for shoes.

* * *

The night was silent and a light breeze cooled the air. The brothers sat in the Red Barn gas station parking lot in a green Pontiac Grand Am. A medium-sized U-Haul was the only other vehicle present until about two minutes ago, when it departed. "Why we can't smoke, bruh?" Gutta wanted badly to spark the blunt he had prerolled but Gotti was against it.

"We gotta be focused. You think these niggas playin? They ain't playing. You say he had a gun when you seen him, right?" The pair laughed at the *Friday* quote.

"Nigga, you stupid."

"Gotta do something to chill. We actually bout to walk out these niggas hood with a bag full of money and a handgun."

"Yeah, shit sound crazy, don't it. All for the love of Gucci, though. That's why we need to hit this blunt." Gotti popped the clip on his Glock out and pushed it back in.

"Man, spark that shit." The brothers puffed heavily on the THC-filled blunt of exotic weed. The effects calmed their nerves.

"Ay, bruh," Gutta called Gotti.

"Yo."

"If we make it out of this shit, I'mma need that two mil."

"For what?"

"I owe Damian."

"You owe Damian? How you end up owing a wild ass Jamaican two million dollars?"

"I don't, I owe him tree."

"Tree?"

"Yeah, that's what he said."

Gotti couldn't help but smile and shake his head. "We gone save that for later. Tell me when we get back to Gucci house."

The alarm on Gutta's phone went off. It was 8:50. Time to show up and show out. Making a right into Aqueduct apartments, Gotti parked the Pontiac at the first building. Both brothers hopped out, carrying Wilson tennis bags. The huge tote bags contained about $100,000 separated between the two. The other bundles were decoys of magazine paper used to give the bag the appearance of being stuffed. Gotti and Gutta wore stone-faced expressions as they moseyed deeper into the apartment complex. Mindful of the inevitable ambush they were walking into, their position was simply kill or die trying.

The appointed meeting spot in the back of the projects was packed with all types of vehicles. This appeased the pair greatly. The variety of vehicles, ranging from Neons to U-Hauls, would serve as perfect cover when the shots start flying. "Torn! We here, bitch nigga! Let's get this shit poppin!" Gutta shouted, observing the numerous apartment windows, looking for any sign of life. "You hear me, nigga! Bring my sister out fore I burn this muthafucka down!"

As if on cue, Torn and Fatts emerged from the hallway with two of their soldiers brandishing pistols. "Damn, nigga, what, you trynna get us evicted?"

Torn's blasé attitude made Gutta's blood boil. "Man, where Gucci at? We got yo bread right here."

"Yeah, let's go ahead and get this out the way cause I don't really like killing all these cute ass females."

"Why you kill my wife then? That shit ain't gangsta, nigga." Gotti couldn't resist asking the question.

"I ain't kill her. You should've paid that bread. You know that ain't even my style."

"Damn shame what happened to that dog," Fatts interjected. Torn's clique burst into laughter. Torn bent over, slapping his leg, hysterical at Fatts' joke.

Gutta was two seconds from pulling his pistol. "Look, y'all playing? What we doing, cause I ain't got all night."

"Aight, aight, hand me that bread."

"You a goddamn lie if you think I'mma just hand you some bread. Let me see my sister first. I don't trust y'all niggas."

Torn nodded. Fatts went to a nearby Infiniti, popping the trunk. Reaching in, he snatched a bound Gucci out by her hair. Her eyes were big as toilet paper rolls. Silently she thanked Jesus for her saviors. "Now toss that bread."

"Soon as you let her go." Fatts released Gucci and the brothers tossed both bags of cash at his feet. Fatts crouched, unzipping the bags. Surveying the cash, he inspected the large bills.

Gotti cut the ropes off Gucci's wrists. He gave her a massive hug. "Run." She took off as fast as her weakened legs could take her.

"Do I gotta count this?"

"Don't matter, you ain't gone live long enough to spend it."

"Speaking of that." Torn raised his fist in the black power salute. Bud caught the signal. From his perch in an adjacent apartment window, he quickly released three shots from his Remington nine-millimeter sniper rifle. Two of the silenced bullets penetrated Gotti's chest. One collided with his cheek as he dropped.

"Bruh!" Gutta's voice boomed through the parking lot. Running to his brother's side, he placed both knees on the ground, cradling his bloody skull. With an anguished expression on his face, he wept.

When he looked up, Torn noticed the scowl of a maniacal psychopath. "Don't worry, you'll be reunited real quick," he said. He bit his bottom lip, aiming his gun at Gutta's nose.

Pop. Without warning Torn's shoulder ripped. The impact caused him to lose grip of his pistol. Suddenly the back door of a medium-sized U-Haul that was parked burst open. Lump, Lil Man, and M.A. hopped out, firing various shots in Torn's direction. Fatts and his two unnamed goons rushed to drag their leader behind a parked Nissan Altima. "Aw, shit." Torn's wound burned like Usher when Chili left.

"You good, my nigga. It's time to show and prove. Suck that shit up." Fatts' back was against the Altima's rear light. His thirst for blood was increasing by the second. Like Tyrese in the movie *Waist Deep*, he mounted the car, sending precision shots from his 17-shot Beretta. *Bok... Bok... Bok...*

"What the—" He was unexpectedly blinded. Tye, Hot Boy, and K.T. sped into the parking lot with the old-school Caprice's high beams on full power. "Round two, bitch." Tye hopped out the driver's door, sending a flurry of bullets towards the Altima. Two slugs entered Fatts' abdomen, ripping holes through his intestines. His body tumbled to the ground.

The sight enraged Torn, compelling him to retaliate. In a blind fury he extended his Desert Eagle around the car's rear end, engulfing the Caprice in rock-sized slugs. Torn's arm shook from the gun's powerful recoil. *Boom... Boom.... Boom.* One of the large shells destroyed K.T.'s face as he exited the vehicle. Aqueduct apartments resembled a Syrian war zone. Shots were being exchanged from all angles. Bullets glided through the residents' walls, forcing them to find refuge in their hall closets and bathrooms. Torn's wound throbbed as he used both hands to steady his gigantic weapon.

Bud was still spying targets through his scope. In the nick of time he caught M.A. creeping behind an unsuspecting Torn. With his finger firmly on the trigger, he steadied his breathing and *Pop.* The slug collided with M.A.'s back, knocking him forward. Tye, Lil Man, and Gutta froze as the life left their childhood friend's body.

"Shit! Shit! Shit!" Gutta strained to suppress his grief. "I got that nigga." Viewing the assassin crouched in the building window, he hustled to the U-Haul, grabbing a Nike book bag from the truck. With the bag in his possession, he sprinted to the building, placing his back against the wall. Carefully he slid directly under the window. On one knee he unzipped the book bag and pulled out a green hand grenade. Removing the pin, he tossed it backwards through the window and took off. Three seconds later... *Kaboom!* The blast could be felt for blocks. Shrapnel bits tore through everything in its path. The gunfire halted.

When the smoke cleared, everybody was discombobulated. Lil Man and Lump were the first to recuperate. Side by side they noticed the opposition's remaining two goons trying to regain their composure. Aiming their pistols, they simultaneously pulled the trigger, placing holes the size of bowling balls in both their foreheads.

Torn was in disbelief. His plan to assassinate his enemies resulted in him losing 90 percent of his top soldiers, including his one true friend, Fatts. Handicapped and outnumbered, he quickly fled to the nearest hallway, bumrushing some stranger's apartment.

Gutta, with his gun drawn, crossed the parking lot. Sirens whirred in the distance. Without warning a black Ford Explorer raced towards him. Like a deer in headlights, he froze. The driver's door opened and Gucci stuck her head out. "Come on, y'all, the cops right behind me." The remaining soldiers jogged to the truck. Gucci pushed the pedal to the floor, fishtailing from the parking lot like Letty in *Fast and Furious.*

* * *

Detectives Brodey and Spider were the first plainclothes officers on the scene. "Unbelievable." Spider was flabbergasted. The entire neighborhood was in shambles. Bullets were stuck in almost every solid object and spent shells covered the ground like rocks in a driveway. Blood and bodies made the parking lot look like the graveyard at a concentration camp. Uniformed officers moved from body to body, checking for pulses. "We got a live one over here."

The detectives hurried to the suspect. "Jaxavier Walker, you lucky son of a bitch." Of all the bodies, Gotti's was the last one he wanted to see alive. The chance to investigate his murder would've been the icing on the cake to the scorned detective.

"Another one! We got another breather!"

Brodey and Spider made their way to the back of a bullet-riddled Nissan Altima. "Wait a minute, don't we know him?" Turlington studied Fatts. "Yeah, Tyriq Hollows. He the one wanted for killing that college student at the gas station a while back."

"Yep, that's him."

"These stupid motherfuckers making our jobs easy. Sooner or later we gone start getting laid off."

"It's a dog-eat-dog world out here, my friend. All we gotta do is put 'em in the cage."

* * *

Angels all over me/Thuggin and lovin the streets/truckin and clutching the heat/I'm bustin they bustin at me/Angels all over me/sick as a dog and I'm hurting/paranoid smoking the purple/on trial and I'm fighting a murda/Angels all ova me. Boosie's lyrics blared through the entertainment system in Gucci's living room. Gutta had stayed over after the draining shootout. The entire house was grief-stricken. Down the hall Ms. Tina and Gucci wept constantly, mourning the death of Gotti. Not able to sleep, Gutta sat up the entire night, using various songs to verbalize his emotions. With his head rested against the back of the sofa, he closed his eyes. Memories of his brother flooded his thoughts. The torment he felt was excruciating.

"Gutta! Gutta!" He shot up, reaching for his pistol. Ms. Tina and Gucci bumrushed the living room. "We gotta go to Riverside now."

"For what?"

"Just come on, hurry up."

The fluorescent lights pained Gutta's eyes as he navigated Riverside's hallways. The receptionist directed him to room 1539. Gucci and Ms. Tina literally jogged down the busy corridor. "Here, here it go." Without warning they entered the hospital room. Gutta's heart sank to the pit of his stomach. Gotti lay still, attached to all kinds of machines. The repetitive beeping of his heart monitor indicated that he was alive. Gutta froze. His eyes were on the brim of tears.

"Thank Jesus! Thank Jesus!" Gucci was bouncing off the walls. "I told you God was good. You see, this ain't a miracle, it's a blessing."

Knock-knock. A Dr. Oz lookalike stood at the door. Ms. Tina rushed to greet him. "Hey, I'm his mother, Tina Walker. Are you the one that saved my son's life?"

"I'm sorry but I can't take credit for that. Besides the loss of blood, there really wasn't much to be done."

"So what happened?"

"It seems he was struck with three bullets, two to his chest and one to the right side of his face. Fortunately he was wearing protective armor under his clothes, stopping the chest shots from penetrating his flesh, and the one to his face passed right through his mouth without hitting any major arteries. So I guess you can say God was just on his side."

"I told you, Gutta." Those words were music to Gucci's ears.

"Why he not awake?" Gutta asked.

"The impact of his head bouncing off the concrete caused trauma to his brain, sending him into a temporary coma. But don't worry, cause it's more likely than not that he will make a full recovery."

"Thanks, Doc."

As the doctor exited, the family congregated beside Gotti's bed. Gutta couldn't help but think of how close he was to losing his soul. His brother was his other half. Without him he would never feel complete.

"We need to pray. Everybody bow y'all heads." With his head lowered, Gutta waited for Gucci to speak, but nothing happened.

"Yo, what's up?"

"I think you should do it, Gutta."

"Come on, sis, just do it."

"Nah, bruh, you have a lot of demons haunting you right now. I see it every time I look at you, and I know you see it too. So it's about time you had a conversation with the Lord."

Not seeing any escape, Gutta bowed his head. Samuel Jackson's Ezekial 25:17 words flowed through him like blood through his veins. "The path of the righteous is beset on all sides by the inequities of the selfish and the tyranny of evil men. Blessed is he who, in the name of charity and good will, shepherds the weak through the valley of darkness for he truly is his brother's keeper. I will strike down upon thee with great vengeance and furious anger those who attempt to poison and destroy my brother. And you will know my name is Gutta when I lay my vengeance upon thee."

ANGELS ALL OVER ME

THE END

www.ingramcontent.com/pod-product-compliance
Lightning Source LLC
Chambersburg PA
CBHW071958040426
42447CB00009B/1394